Some Poems
and Some Talk
about Poetry

Some Poems
and Some Talk
about Poetry

by
Frank Manley
and
Floyd C. Watkins

UNIVERSITY PRESS OF MISSISSIPPI
Jackson

Manufactured in the United States of America

All poems in this book have been reprinted from *Resultances* by Frank Manley by permission of the University of Missouri Press. Copyright 1980 by Frank Manley.

Library of Congress Cataloging in Publication Data

Manley, Frank.
    Some poems and some talk about poetry

    1. Manley, Frank—Interviews.   2. Poets, American—
20th century—Interviews.   3. Poetry—Authorship.
4. Poetry.   I. Watkins, Floyd C.   II. Title.
PS3563.A517Z475   1985   811'.54   84-13061
ISBN 0-87805-230-5

In Memory of Our Parents

Acknowledgments

For various kinds of assistance and encouragement in the writing and preparation of this book we are much indebted to Trudy Kretchman, Helen Fontseré, William B. Dillingham, Watkins's class in Southern Literature, Special Collections of the Woodruff Library of Emory University. Richard Marius, of Harvard University, kindly read the manuscript and offered perceptive suggestions. Our wives, Anna Watkins and Carolyn Manley, encouraged and helped. Emory University, particularly Dean Ellen Mickiewicz and Dean David Minter, was especially generous in financial support.

Contents

A Critic and a Poet in Search of a Preface

The Critic

This is a book about writing poetry and reading it and also a book about talking about the writing and reading of poetry.

In this volume the reader (or interviewer and asker of questions) is Floyd Watkins, a native of a small town in north Georgia, hillman, kinsman of farmers and men from the country, occasional farmer himself. After a quarter of a century of life in a small town, teaching in a public school in south Georgia, three years in what was once called the Army Air Corps at bases in Alaska and the Aleutians, Watkins followed the typical pattern of what has been called the greatest migration in all history—the move from town and country to city in America after World War II. Watkins fell into the city. He completed his education, became a teacher of American literature (especially regional and southern) at Emory University, and stayed in the city. He could not move the university back to the country; so he became an unconverted city-dweller with occasional sojourns in the country.

Frank Manley, the poet in this volume, was born to the ways of the city, Atlanta. He commuted by streetcar to get an education in some English literature, a great deal of Latin, and some Greek. He studied at Johns Hopkins and taught at Yale. He wrote books and articles on John Donne, Shakespeare and other Elizabethans, and Saint Thomas More. But books and northern universities did not provide a full life for Manley, who returned to the South, Atlanta, and Emory. Manley established the pattern of his own life, and chance and character led to ways of living as various as those of a well-rounded Renaissance man. Sometimes with family or friend, sometimes alone, Manley camped, fished, carved wood and stone, worked with stained glass, hunted Indian artifacts, and wrote articles and books about archaeology and literature. He began to want space, and often talked with Watkins about buying a house or home or place in the country.

Then Watkins's brother, a physician in a north Georgia country town, moved to the city. He owned a farm with trees, cattle, pasture, apple trees, stone walls, and, as the realtors say, a bold mountain spring. A dilapidated farm house, built in the 1920s, was used as a place for storing hay. So Manley bought the farm and began to reverse the pattern of the greatest migration in history. One summer he lived on the farm without electricity or plumbing. Over a few years he dug a privy, wired the house, rebuilt the porch and the chimney, cleared a garden and fields of hay, and began, simultaneously, to write poetry about his childhood, Roman emperors and men of the Renaissance, his own wife and children, and neighbors he had come to know in the country.

Finally Manley employed an architect and contractors to remodel extensively and expand the old country home. Still regarding himself as mainly a citizen of Atlanta, he sold his city home, moved to the country, and commuted to the University to teach. A Catholic, he sometimes attended the country churches and marveled at the rhetoric and gestures of the country preachers. He visited and talked with his neighbors, mended the stone fences of his farm, went to the cemetery cleanings on Decoration Day at the country churches, and continued to study modern poets, classical writings, and Renaissance literature. He taught and wrote articles and books and poems. He searched through continents and ages for literature, art, and subjects for his scholarship and his poetry. He collected his poems, published them in a volume called *Resultances* (a title suggested by Donne), and won the Devins Award for poetry.

In the meanwhile, Watkins read Manley's poems as they appeared in one periodical and then another. He searched for variety and change and for a poet known personally to his students in southern literature. Manley's poems offered excellence and an author and teacher who demonstrates to the students that someone they know writes poetry. From the poets Watkins taught in the course (John Crowe Ransom, Robert Penn Warren, Allen Tate, James Dickey), he dropped Tate. Watkins knew the backgrounds of the poems about Atlanta and north Georgia, but he did not know the origins of the classical poems; often he did not know the poems themselves well even when they were about his own country and after he had read them many times. So Manley consented to interviews and talk and readings. The two talked about some poems and Watkins then taught them, stating both Manley's views and his own when they disagreed. Watkins—as teacher in charge—chose the poems he wanted but sometimes graciously—as he thought—allowed Manley to pick one from a range or a selection of two. Usually poet and interviewer talked about a poem and then Watkins taught it; sometimes the two talked about a poem which had already been studied in class. Again, the two talked about a poem before the class and on tape recorder without planning, preparation, or rehearsal.

An interview, a good one at least, is a new and strange experience for the poet and the critic. With trembling and fear of ignorance, the interviewer asks for the meanings of allusions, the devices of the poetic art of a work, the sources of the poems themselves. The poet reaches into the details of the poem for bits of information never dreamed of by the reader. It is a surprise to the interviewer when the maker of a poem tells him that he does not himself know the answer. It is a surprise too when the poet admits that the reader's discovered truth in the poem is true to the work and its meanings even when the poet was not rationally aware of that content at the time of composition. The reader is surprised that a poet can be told something he does not know about his own poem. On the other hand, the poet's answer may make the reader shockingly aware of his own error, insensitivity, and ignorance.

Ultimately, a poem is its own self. It is greater than the writer at any given moment during the creation of the poem or of his life. It draws from plans, intuition, association, corners and crevices of the poet's experience utterly unknown to the reader, sometimes momentarily or consciously forgotten by the poet. All personal and impersonal experience, intimate and vicarious, rushes in on the poet as he sometimes laboriously and sometimes impulsively plants or hastily strews the words on the page. A poem may *mean* and it may *be,* but seldom or never does a good poem exist in all its fulness in any single moment. That is its ultimate mystery, never fully fathomed by poet or reader, never fully revealed in any moment of reading or any interview.

The main point to be made about these interviews is that they are simply easy conversations between friends. They were fun to do, despite Watkins's trying to pin me down, and I hope they are fun for others to read. I am thinking of passages such as this:

> **Watkins:** Did you ever at the time realize that you're moving closer and closer to home when you go from New Guinea to Guatemala to Cuba to Savannah?
> **Manley:** I never noticed that. No. But I believe it.
> **Watkins:** Is it meaningful?
> **Manley:** Oh, yes. Indeed it is.
> **Watkins:** Do you know when I noticed it? Just now.
> **Manley:** Well, you got me beat. I never noticed it at all.

Or the story Watkins tells about his Uncle Bud Wheeler, who was drunk one night preaching a sermon, saying, "Here I sit on my mule preaching the gospel. If I'd had the chance I'd a been a damn good preacher." Or Watkins's fear of alarm clocks or his abilities as a preacher himself, gasping under the inspiration of the Holy Spirit, or his distress on learning that people in the mountains decorate the graves of their dead with plastic flowers and love the garish unnaturalness of them and his concern that they not be laughed at, that a man can be illiterate and un-educated and still think and feel as deeply as anyone else, or his lumbering jokes about my sex life and Erasmus's or his refer-ences to Faulkner's Benjy and Vardaman, which come to him as naturally as the leaves on a tree, having taught Faukner every year of his life for the last thirty years. These are very human interviews, and much of what makes them as warm and accessi-ble as they are is Watkins's genuineness and the openness, hon-esty, and force of his personality.

Watkins's main job was to ask questions. It is a role he is particularly suited for, having done in generations of students with questions fired at them faster than they can think, forcing them out of abstractions into the particular, the concrete, the graphic, the elemental—asking questions where one does not even realize a question exists until Watkins leads him into it and he discovers he is trapped. Watkins handles questions the same way an experienced craftsman handles the tools of his trade. What is a ghost, he asks at one point, and I am halfway through a reply before I realize I do not know. I do not even believe in ghosts. His role is to pin me down, make me explain myself, make me precise. He does not flinch from anything. "What do you mean by 'the breasts you point'?" he asks about "Erasmus in Love."

Manley: Just that some breasts are pointy breasts.
Watkins: Who has "cupped them in his hands"?
Manley: Erasmus.
Watkins: How about the poet?
Manley: No, the poet's not there. This is just Erasmus.
Watkins: Are you being prudish, now?
Manley: No, no. This is in the poem; that's Erasmus.

"Who's speaking," he asks at another point in the same poem:

Manley: I am, the poet.
Watkins: But it's not the poet; it's the persona; you're not back in Erasmus's time.
Manley: No, except for the fact that I imagined Erasmus to be in that time, and therefore I'm there too.
Watkins: So you put yourself imaginatively in that room and you see Erasmus stare across the room at you.
Manley: Erasmus saw the woman, because he was writing about the woman; so I see Erasmus because I am writing about Erasmus. And if I see Erasmus, Erasmus sees me.
Watkins: There are a lot of remarkable steps of the imagination here.

The last line was said, I am sure, with some wonder and with a measure of scepticism and doubt.

But if it is Watkins's job to ask the questions—as it is the job of any critic or reader—it is my job as poet to evade them as best I can and insist on the integrity and wholeness of the experience and its being allowed to resist normal strictures of logic. "Is there an actual unbottoning of the blouse," Watkins asks of the same poem, "or is that in his mind?"

Manley: It's hard, I think, to tell what's happening and what isn't happening in the poem. I imagined this to be happening in his mind.
Watkins: Who does the unbottoning?
Manley: She does it after he writes that she does it (laughs)—if that makes any sense. He creates her to do it, and then she does it. What I wanted to do was have the reader not know, Floyd, and the kind of question you're asking is the kind of question I don't want the poem to answer. I want people to wonder.
Watkins: Am I reading it wrongly or rightly by wondering?
Manley: You're absolutely right in wondering, but I think you can't get an answer.
Watkins: Okay. I'll buy that.

The same thing happens over and over. In the poem "Ghost" there is a question as to the identity of the ghost.

Watkins: Well, is he the ghost?
Manley: Yes.
Watkins: I disagree. (Laughter).
Manley: (Laughter.) Well, he's the *main* ghost.
Watkins: You ought to have made the title plural.
Manley: "Ghosts"? Well, I guess I should have.
Watkins: Don't joke with me. You really admit that?
Manley: Well, no, I like "Ghost," period. One ghost. I think what I'm talking about is singular. I'm talking about being made into a ghost.
Watkins: I was taking the ghost as the poet or the persona.
Manley: Right.
Watkins: The persona is not Ben Mathis.
Manley: Yes.
Watkins: What's happening in the first three lines?
Manley: All right, it's a conflation of the two . . . (Laughter.)

Here he pins me down. By keeping after me and not letting me off with an easy answer, he forces me to admit the conflation I obviously had in mind when I first wrote the poem. And yet in a sense we're both right. There is only one ghost because the two have come together, and there is no need to try to separate them and say this line refers to Ben Mathis and this other one to the speaker of the poem. I wanted the central image of a ghost because I wanted the ambivalence, the essential ambiguity a ghost would suggest. I was not thinking in the same discreet terms Watkins wanted me to describe it in. And yet his insistence on knowing precisely, on seeing it clearly and getting it straight, forces me to dredge up things that I am aware of only in a different way, on a different level of consciousness, which I then try to translate or articulate in a more discursive fashion.

Again and again in these interviews I seem to be discovering things about my poems that I never knew before. But it is not a question of that, for there are different ways of knowing, and not all of them are articulate or even fully conscious. Nor need they be. My wife is fond of saying that everyone already knows everything anyway, by which she means that people never fool one another, that we pick up things about one another beyond what is said through nuances, subtleties, suggestions of meaning that far exceed the calculations of the conscious mind to explain them. In the discussion of "Retardation Center" there is a question of what is meant by the phrase "hangs in a hug." Watkins had the idea that the people in the poem were hugging themselves. I thought they were hugging one another. "I was thinking not necessarily of the straight jacket," Watkins says, "but of one so much retarded and within himself, he closes his arms and his eyes and hangs within himself, hugging himself."

> **Manley:** That's a wonderful way to look at the line. It's not what I had in mind, but I think it would certainly be there in the words.
>
> **Watkins:** That is to say, you are pleased to have in the poem the concept of the complete outgoingness of hanging together and also the ambivalence of the complete innerness of hugging oneself. . . . Now is this a random bumping together or is this a deliberate *going* together and a feeling of love?
>
> **Manley:** Well, I don't know. It doesn't really say what it is. I had the blind and the deaf groping, trying to come into contact with something, and then I had the next line "hanging in a hug."
>
> **Watkins:** But it's not what "*it*" says; it's what the author says, isn't it?
>
> **Manley:** I don't have a definite memory of what I intended when I wrote it, and I'm not certain it would be all that important even if I had.
>
> **Watkins:** One thing I hope we both are saying about poetry is that there is a great deal of effort required for poetry, but once one makes the effort, he is bound to hit a lot of lucky things. They're not God-given, but they're not artistic accomplishments, just lucky successes.

Now I don't believe that. I don't believe in lucky successes. I don't believe that poetry consists only in what's earned by the poet's conscious effort and that anything beyond that, any dimly perceived, preconscious, or as yet inarticulate meaning or emotional state is not to be regarded as part of the same creative flow or process, no matter when one discovers it, while the poem is still going on or six months or six years later. And put in those terms, I'm sure Watkins would agree. Part of the difference between us here is the difference in roles. Watkins asks questions of me as though I were a traveler returned from a strange land, and I respond and explain what I saw there. But after the poem is over, the poet is no longer part of the experience. He stands outside it like any other reader trying to explain what he sees there. That is why some poets are better at talking about their poetry than others. Their critical faculties are more developed, they are more used to thinking in discursive terms. But during the actual act of writing they are all equal. Things occur beyond their knowing. Levels of consciousness are brought into play that one is only dimly aware of. Poets have always spoken of the experience of being lifted up and having something speak through them, the words forming beyond their own ability to phrase them. I am reminded of F. Scott Fitzgerald. Late in his marriage when his wife Zelda was no longer able to live in the world and was institutionalized at Ashville, she told him she envied his talent as a writer. She had tried dancing and painting and writing and had found no escape from what Hopkins calls her "sweating self." She had no means of self-expression. And he told her that he did not express himself through his novels, but that some dark necessity expressed itself through him. And the same is true in their own insignificant way in these poems. Having written them, I now stand apart from them and marvel not at what I have done, but at the beauty and wonder and grandeur of the great forces of creation that men like Teilhard de Chardin tell us are still going on in us and through us and by us and in the universe itself all around us.

Puzzlings

Dead Letters

The safety deposit box
Had a hole in it
Plugged up
With a note that said
There wasn't anything here in the first place

And that was it
Except for some used furniture
Only a drunk would haul away
Or St. Vincent de Paul's
Or a drunk working for St. Vincent de Paul's

I cleaned out the apartment
Had the mail forwarded
The unpaid last few months of his life
And then one night on the parapet—

No.
That's not right.
          That was later.

The first letter I got from my father
After he died
Was from New Guinea
It said
The natives are starving Frank
Waiting for parachutes
Send five dollars
Quick

A week later from Guatemala
The letter said
This is no vacation Frank
I am in the mountains
With Camilo Torres
We have bombed the President's Palace
We sleep in ancient ruins
And wait for government trucks to pass
Send five dollars in care of the Melvilles

In Cuba
In Cuernavaca with Ivan Illich
In Baltimore at Jonah House
My father was there
Shuffling to Selma
Paying bond
Hustling votes in Mississippi
Getting killed and buried under a dam
Walking down a road alone
Tar hot under his feet
The do-rag tied in knots on his head
Waiting for the sniper

While ten nuns in Savannah Georgia
Discalced Carmelites eighty years old
Were praying in shifts
Perpetually
Twenty-four hours a day
For the repose of his soul
My father among them scribbling furiously

Send more money Frank
Wire it collect
Write a check on the back of this holy picture
On the calendar
Count the days of your life

The poor are bleeding to death
The poor are starving Frank
The poor are in jail with no one to help them
The children are dying Frank
They are brain damaged

They are burned to death in frying pans
By parents
Who were burned to death in frying pans
They are beaten by fathers
Who can't find work
While all the cars in the world
Creep up on New York City
The cars are brain damaged Frank
Send five dollars

Quick
Here's a scapular
Three hundred and sixty-five Masses a year
Visits to the Blessed Sacrament
Novenas   litanies
Thirty years plenary indulgence

In every letter to the dead
From every otherworldly
Catholic charity
He ever sent five dollars to
My father's restless spirit
Roams the world
Crying
List list oh list

Like the other night on the parapet
Rumors of invasion
A blood-red moon
Carousing in the palace

Far below
Silence   darkness
And there beyond the battlements
The very shape and gesture of his thought
He spoke to me in his native tongue

I could a tale unfold
He said
Whose lightest word
Would harrow up thy soul
Freeze thy young blood
Make thy two eyes
Like stars
To start from their spheres
Thy knotted and combined locks to part
And each particular hair
To stand on end
Like quills upon the fretful porcupine
But this eternal blazon must not be
To ears of flesh and blood
List list oh list
If ever thou didst thy dear father love
Send five dollars

And I said
In the same language
Rest, rest, perturbéd spirit
But I thought to myself
Oh cursed spite that ever I was born to set it right
And then I thought
Nay

Come
Let's go together

Finally, Charity Abideth

Watkins: Is this poem unusually personal and autobiographical?

Manley: Yes. It's more about me than my father.

Watkins: Aren't you more open about personal poems than most poets? Frost wouldn't say anything about his. He would never read his "Home Burial" to audiences.

Manley: If I choose to make an experience public, then I've objectified it enough to talk about it. It took me a while to learn to write about some areas in my life. When I first began, I could only write about certain things. And then I could write about a few more, and then a few more. Maybe if I kept writing, I could write about all of it.

Watkins: Are any of your poems too personal for you to talk about?

Manley: Maybe. I don't think this one is.

Watkins: In what sense are the letters "dead"?

Manley: They are like letters coming from the dead. The postal service also uses the term to signify letters that can't be delivered. They end up in some place in the post office.

Watkins: Those are lost letters. The people may be living, but they're not findable. That's the dead letter office.

Manley: I wanted to write about letters not getting to the person they were sent to. These letters were sent to my father when he was dead, and they didn't get to him. Therefore they were dead letters, but they were also like letters coming from him, from the dead, to me.

Watkins: They're dead to your father because he's dead, but when they are forwarded to you they live again in you.

Manley: Right.

Watkins: When did your father die?

Manley: About 1970, I think.

Watkins: How long after your father was dead did you write this poem?

Manley: Oh, some while, maybe four, five, six, seven years—something like that.

Watkins: Then you remembered and maybe even experienced emotional reactions—grief—for six or seven years?

Manley: I suppose so, and I kept getting these letters all that time. I *still* get some, and that's been twelve years ago.

Watkins: I found that grief for a parent was for me not as intense at the time of death as it was sustained over a long period of years.

Manley: I don't know whether "grief" is the word for it. I still think about my father a lot. It isn't something you actually forget because your parents really do live in you.

Watkins: Until recently, I would find myself shaving and say, "Now, I'm gonna tell Dad that."

Manley: Sometimes when I am shaving I think, "Don't I look like my father?" The older I get the more I think my jaw looks a lot like my father's.

Watkins: These are a certain kind of letters. What kind are they? Who are they from?

Manley: Junk mail. Religious junk mail. These are all requests from Catholic charities run by various religious orders that my father contributed to. He got on their mailing list.

Watkins: Is Catholicism itself the subject of the poem?

Manley: Very much so. Almost everything in here is a reference to Catholicism.

Watkins: How are you different from your father? How do you react to such letters? Did he send money?

Manley: Yes.

Watkins: Would you?

Manley: No. I don't think I have as simple a faith as my father did. My father really believed everything the church taught, and he tried to be a good citizen of the church. I'm not a good citizen at all. I don't believe everything the church teaches; and I don't have the simple kind of piety that my parents had. He had a kind of uneducated, unreflective response.

Watkins: But genuine.

Manley: Genuine, yes. My father gave to Catholic charities because he felt he was doing good. I admire that. But I think that the people he gave to, a lot of them, weren't necessarily doing that much good.

Watkins: You appreciate then his attitude toward religious benevolence?

Manley: Yes. But the charities I mention are not the ones my father contributed to. They're ones I'm interested in.

Watkins: What does the first stanza mean?

> The safety deposit box
> Had a hole in it
> Plugged up
> With a note that said
> There wasn't anything here in the first place.

Manley: My father wasn't a very rich man. That's what I meant.

Watkins: Did he have a safety deposit box?

Manley: Yes.

Watkins: Did you open it?

Manley: My sister and I did.

Watkins: What did you find?

Manley: Not much. You know, some family papers. A little bit of this and that and the other. But not much.

Watkins: So the note that said there wasn't anything here in the first place did not exist. It's an invention.

Manley: Right. What I'm suggesting in that first stanza is that everything's drained out of the safety deposit box, but there wasn't anything there anyway to drain out. It's just a statement that my father didn't have much money.

Watkins: On how many occasions have you been through the effects of a dead person?

Manley: Just my father's.

Watkins: Not your mother's?

Manley: No.

Watkins: I did it once for a friend and once for my mother and then for my father. It's an overwhelming experience. Did you find it so?

Manley: I really did.

Watkins: You communicate that in the poem. Did going through those effects and getting those letters change your attitude toward your father?

Manley: Yes, indeed. I discovered something I didn't know about my father.

Watkins: What was that?

Manley: That he was giving money to these charities.

Watkins: And you saw more benevolence and goodness in your father than ever before?

Manley: More than I'd known was there.

Watkins: This is a contradiction to a lot of other literature in which one finds terrible secrets in the effects of the dead, an illegitimate half-brother or something.

Manley: Yes. You find that in literature and in your own family too.

Watkins: What's the technical form of this poem?

Manley: Free verse.

Watkins: All the stanzas are different and I believe adapted to the form of the irregular ode.

Manley: That's interesting.

Watkins: Technically and metrically an irregular ode is free verse, isn't it?

Manley: Yes. I would not be uncomfortable calling it an irregular ode.

Watkins: Allen Tate's "Ode to the Confederate Dead" and Wordsworth's "Ode on the Intimations of Immortality" both have every stanza different, and your poem has the high seriousness of an irregular ode. It is rather modern in being a very private irregular ode. Now your second stanza says, "And that was it." Since there was nothing in the safety deposit box, no possessions, that was true. But it's also ironic, isn't it? In the light of everything else that occurs in the poem there's a hell of a lot more.

Manley: Yes. What this poem is about is the inheritance I received from my father. There was no material inheritance, but what I discover in the course of the poem is that there was another kind of inheritance.

Watkins: When did you change your mind about your father? Was it during the six or seven years after his death and before the writing of the poem?

Manley: The poem is a dramatic presentation of what happened over a long period of time in my life.

Watkins: The change in the course of the poem is therefore also the change in the course of your life.

Manley: Right. I am trying to talk about certain responses to the world that I inherited from my father. The poem shows what's happening dramatically.

Watkins: You have said rather uncomplimentary things about your father.

Manley: Yes.

Watkins: Have you changed your attitude toward those?

Manley: They coexist.

Watkins: They coexisted in him, as good and evil do in every one. You just learned more about the existence of the good.

Manley: That's right. And I learned more about myself.

Watkins: What is St. Vincent de Paul's?

Manley: A charitable organization in the Catholic Church. They have stores in poor sections of town that sell used clothing and furniture for minimal sums or else give things away. Usually they have poor, destitute people helping out. It's very much like the Salvation Army.

Watkins: What is the point about the drunk working for St. Vincent de Paul's?

Manley: Like the Salvation Army, they get a lot alcoholics, people that are down and out in their lives. They are poor guys suffering from hangovers trying to carry a sofa down ten flights of stairs.

Watkins: Do you find looking at that drunk working for St. Vincent de Paul's humorous or pathetic?

Manley: A little of both. Again, it's a way of saying that my father had nothing. You had to be drunk to haul away some of the stuff my father had.

Watkins: Are you flippant?

Manley: Yes.

Watkins: So at this time you hadn't come to cope with the seriousness.

Manley: No. Maybe the first few stanzas express—or should express—a kind of distance and bitterness and the sense that the speaker is saying, "Well, I didn't really get any inheritance here. My father left me nothing. He had nothing, and he passed nothing on to me." There is this distant, flip attitude.

Watkins: The third stanza:

> The first letter I got from my father
> After he died

Was from New Guinea
It said
The natives are starving Frank
Waiting for parachutes
Send five dollars
Quick

Is that said in horror or matter of factly, indicating a lack of emotion?

Manley: I meant that to be straightforward.

Watkins: You are so objective that there's no grief in you, no pity for the natives of New Guinea.

Manley: A little. Not much.

Watkins: So this is, then, also a semihumorous stanza, where you don't yet take seriously your father's charities.

Manley: Well, the sense of charity builds in the poem. But here at the beginning I'm just referring to the Cargo Cult. It's a factual reference. In World War II, the natives in New Guinea saw parachutes falling from the sky with all sorts of supplies, and they thought it was God sending them blessings. After the war was over, they would get together and pray that the airplanes would return and drop more parachutes, and they developed a religion called the Cargo Cult. The only place in there that points to the direction the rest of the poem takes are the lines "The natives are starving Frank / Waiting for parachutes."

Watkins: I find it also in the "Quick."

Manley: Right. The urgency. The speaker is not aware yet of the way the poem is going to go. You're right, the urgency of the sense of compassion, the need for charity, the need for these starving natives to get something—that's the sort of thing developed later in the poem. Here it's just presented more objectively.

Watkins: Explain the line about the parapet.

Manley: Yes. That's in the third stanza. "I cleaned out the apartment / Had the mail forwarded / The unpaid last few months of his life / And then one night on the parapet—" That's a reference that was just thrown in there and then picked up later in the poem.

Watkins: What is a parapet?

Manley: The battlements of a castle. It's a reference to *Hamlet*. I start to move toward *Hamlet*, and then I say, No—that came later. That's not right.

Watkins: What is the parapet in *Hamlet,* Frank?

Manley: It's where the ghost of Hamlet's father appears.

Watkins: The later reference in your poem is again to the ghost?

Manley: That's right. Here I start to say that his ghost appears to me, and then I say, no, his ghost didn't come until later. First there were these letters.

Watkins: What were "The unpaid last few months of his life"?

Manley: It's a fairly factual reference. The person who is dying doesn't really pay any bills the last few months of his life.

Watkins: And you found all the bills.

Manley: I found all the bills. They had to be paid. The first three stanzas introduce the sense of my closing down my father's life—doing what I had to do and realizing that there was no material inheritance forthcoming. Then I begin to say something about what happened on the parapet but check myself because I realize that came later. Other things came first.

Watkins: Why begin with a letter from New Guinea?

Manley: I just made that up. There are no Catholic charities in New Guinea. I thought this first image of the parachute drifting down is a good image of charity and of the way people need charity. They're starving. They need help quick.

Watkins: I think there's another element in that. I believe the remoteness of New Guinea shows the remoteness of the whole feeling and emotion and of what is later the climax or ending of the poem. It's remote from you at this point. New Guinea is placed so far from the reader that you may have picked it for that reason.

Manley: That's very perceptive. You're probably right. I hadn't thought of that.

Watkins: If you hadn't thought of it, how could it be true?

Manley: (Laughs.) Well, there are a lot of things I haven't thought of that are true.

Watkins: Was it just a lucky choice or was it an intuitive choice?

Manley: I think it was an intuitive choice.

Watkins: Did you ever at the time realize that you're moving closer and closer to home when you go from New Guinea to Guatemala to Cuba to Savannah?

Manley: I never noticed that. No. But I believe it.

Watkins: Is it meaningful?

Manley: Oh, yes. Indeed it is.

Watkins: Do you know when I noticed it? Just now.

Manley: Well, you got me beat. I never noticed it at all.

Watkins: Isn't that why truly great literature may always contain something nobody has ever seen? Therefore we can justify the role of critic. Shall we look and see how it goes on?

Manley: It goes to New York.

Watkins: It gets personal, doesn't it?

Manley: Then it goes to the parapet.

Watkins: Yes, but ultimately it goes to Frank and his father. Explain the stanza about Guatemala and bombing the president's palace.

Manley: That's a reference to guerilla activity in Latin America. I just used Guatemala as a typical example.

Watkins: Guerillas in Latin America. You mean the ones trying to overthrow the government in El Salvador? What does that have to do with the Catholic Church?

Manley: A lot. What I'm referring to here is Liberation Theology—the idea that the church should not hold itself aloof from the world as it has in the past, but should engage itself in the world and help try to make it a better place.

Watkins: I don't see what that has to do with helping guerillas overthrow the government.

Manley: If we try to live lives in agreement with what we believe and we see that the society in which we live deprives its members of enough food to eat and proper sanitation and housing and medical care so that more children die than survive to become adults and there is no work and no education and no hope for anything better, then it is one's moral duty to overthrow the government that creates such a society and establish a new one in its place based on the real needs of its people. It's simply a matter of social justice. If society is breaking up, as it is in Central America, and there are sides to be chosen, it is necessary to be on the side of the poor. Compassion and charity must mean something. One can hardly choose the oppressors.

Watkins: Who is Camillo Torres? Who are the Melvilles?

Manley: Camillo Torres was a Catholic priest who became a Revolutionary in Colombia and was killed. The Melvilles are Americans—Maryknolls, I believe—who were sent to

Guatemala and became radicalized at the injustices they saw. They were sent back to this country and joined Daniel Berrigan in protesting American involvement in Viet Nam. I'm talking here about all the Catholic clergy who have become involved in Latin America in the struggle of the people to free themselves—the archbishop who was machine-gunned in El Salvador, the American nuns who were killed there by government troops, the priests who now hold cabinet positions in the socialist government of Nicaragua. The countries of Latin America are Catholic. The people look to the church for help. The guerillas in each country in Central America are looking for the same thing—a better life for themselves and their people. They're trying to change an oppressive social structure. It just so happened that that social structure is capitalistic, and so it gets thrown into the arena of larger international politics. Basically they're just poor people—destitute people—who are trying to get out from under the crushing poverty that they've experienced all their lives. Most of them are illiterate Indians who make no more than three hundred dollars a year.

Watkins: You are an admirer of Castro?

Manley: Yes, I admire him. I admire him in part because of my religious convictions.

Watkins: But Castro is antireligious, is he not?

Manley: I don't know that he is. I don't know to what degree Castro is a pure Marxist. And I don't know to what degree Cuba is a godless Communistic society, but I suspect it isn't. I think that the Catholic Church has been very influential in the attempt to liberate and bring social justice to Latin America. That's one of the things the poem is about.

Watkins: I feel completely sympathetic to your aims. But I don't want to sleep in the same bed with the people you're sleeping with. Don't you have reservations about that?

Manley: Some. Not too many.

Watkins: What's Jonah House?

Manley: Jonah House is a place in Baltimore where Philip Berrigan, one of the Vietnam protestors, set up a community.

Watkins: You put your own beliefs and causes in your father's letters.

Manley: Exactly. That's right. I pretend that all the letters I got from him were letters having to do with the causes I'm interested in and the way in which I would like to see the world change. Actually the letters I got were much different.

Watkins: In the stanza on the Discalced Carmelites, what does "discalced" mean?

Manley: It means "barefoot." It's a Latin word for "barefoot."

Watkins: As a form of penance.

Manley: Yes. This is a cloistered order of nuns. They go into the monastery or the nunnery and never come out. They wear heavy woolen robes and big leather belts. There really is a Discalced Carmelite nunnery in Savannah, inhabited by only about ten nuns. A friend who was once a nun there said they were very strange women. Most of them are in their eighties.

Watkins: What's the relation between your father and the dead letters and the Discalced Carmelites?

Manley: The tone of the poem is mixed. I want it to be exaggerated and humorous and serious too, all at the same time. The nuns here are exhibiting a form of old-fashioned piety in praying for my father's soul after his death, and he's sitting among them writing letters. They don't even know he's there.

Watkins: Are they a joke to you altogether?

Manley: Well, there is a kind of piety in Catholicism that seems to me extreme, and I can't take it too seriously. I think I can sympathize with the people who feel it, but I myself can't feel it. People like Teilhard de Chardin said that your obligation and duty is to take up the world's business, not to withdraw from it. The world needs a continuing process of creation. I'm contrasting the kind of piety that withdraws from the world with the kind of piety that moves toward it.

Watkins: Dramatically this is a sort of a broken back poem for me, and I have not been able to bring the two parts together yet. On your part there is a new love, a new compassion, and new understanding, along with a continuing recognition that we all have of our fathers' weaknesses. I had never seen anything in this poem except *your* new realization of your father's benevolences and charities. And now you lead me off into all your social thinking.

Manley: The point of linkage is the concept of charity in the sense of doing for someone else, of exhibiting love and concern and compassion for someone else. That's something I didn't know about my father, that he was a charitable man. One of the things about the Catholic Church I like a lot is that good works are important—the corporal works of mercy, to clothe the naked and feed the hungry and bury the dead. The aspect of the church that engages in the needs of the world is something that really fills me with great hope and love.

Watkins: The complexity here, it seems to me, is that you're joking, and you recognize the dead seriousness of the Discalced Carmelites, and it's not all joke.

Manley: That's right. I wanted to make a serious statement, but at the same time treat it lightly.

Watkins: What is the "native tongue"?

Manley: I'm quoting Shakespeare, and almost everything from that point on is a quotation from *Hamlet* that I've just rearranged. I wanted to indicate that it was a foreign language.

Watkins: Is it also related to the unknown tongues of the charismatic movement?

Manley: Yes, I think so. It's also related to the fact that my father has come back from the dead, and he's speaking now as a ghost.

Watkins: And the "native" therefore means dead also.

Manley: Yes. He's speaking that other language used by the dead. But all of that is a quotation from *Hamlet*.

Watkins: What is the quotation?

Manley: "I could a tale unfold whose lightest word / Would harrow up thy soul, freeze thy young blood, / Make thy two eyes, like stars, to start from their spheres, / Thy knotted and combined locks to part / And each particular hair to stand on end / Like quills upon the fretful porpentine. / But this eternal blazon must not be / To ears of flesh and blood. List, list, oh, list! / If ever thou didst thy dear father love—"

Watkins: What does the "list, list, oh, list" mean?

Manley: "Listen, listen, oh listen."

Watkins: I see. I took the "list, list, oh list" as a listing of charities.

Manley: Well, it does. It does mean that. That's exactly what it means.

Watkins: But did it to you at the time?

Manley: I don't remember, but it certainly does when I look at it now. That's exactly what it's talking about. And then, of course, my addition was the "Send five dollars." Here I deflate the splendor of the language and at the same time make the point that I've been making. Hamlet's father's ghost came back and said, "I have been murdered." You don't expect the ghost to come back and say, "Send five dollars." And yet that's exactly what the ghost has been saying.

Watkins: When your father is constantly calling on *you* to perform charities, do you feel a familial obligation?

Manley: Yes.

Watkins: Did you send any money?

Manley: Yes. But it's difficult because my idea of what charity should be is different from my father's. I would send money somewhere different from where he would. Like in the passage here: "a scapular / Three hundred and sixty-five Masses a year." What they do is give you a "spiritual bouquet," as they call it. They send you a little pamphlet or brochure from some obscure monastery out in the Midwest and say they will say a mass for you every day of the year if you send five dollars.

Watkins: I'll bet it's a quick one.

Manley: That's right. It's *quid pro quo.* We'll make a spiritual bouquet for you, we'll say three Our Fathers, two Hail Mary's and Glory Be to the Father's every day for two hundred and fifty years if you send us so much money. It's the same aspect of the church that Martin Luther objected to—selling prayers. My sense of charity is not to give five dollars to these various causes but the idea that charity is important to the world. That is the burden that was laid on me—the idea that I ought to, in my best self, do something for other people. This is my inheritance; this is what was given to me by my father.

Watkins: And so you were born to set it right.

Manley: That's right. (Laughs.)

Watkins: Where does the figure, the image, the symbol of frying pans come from?

Manley: I think I made it up myself. I don't remember anyone really *frying* a child like that. I wanted to indicate that children are afflicted in this way by their parents, and their parents in their time were afflicted in the same way by their parents. They pass it on. I guess it's a kind of inheritance. The same way I was passed on something by my father, they were passed on something by their parents.

Watkins: Why in the world did you switch from children to brain-damaged cars, Frank?

Manley: I thought the whole society was brain-damaged, and the cars are just a sign of that. Something is really wrong with our society when cars start creeping around on their own. Cars don't have brains, of course, but if they did they'd go down the highway like they're supposed to. They wouldn't go creeping up on New York City.

Watkins: Which was transcendent at the time of the writing of the poem, your poetic thinking or your emotional thinking of your father and the need for compassion and charity? Do they completely meld, or are you a technical poet standing back looking at what you're doing?

Manley: To me, they meld. I mean, this was all complex emotion, thought, feeling—all one thing. And it came out very quickly.

Watkins: You are beginning to show me something about yourself as a poet. Many poets are not as intuitive as you are. I'm thinking of a poet whose manuscripts I've looked at who listed fifteen rhymes for one word on his manuscript.

Manley: No, this poem is very intuitive. Others are not. Some poems come very quickly. Others require a lot of labor. This one is just about the way I first wrote it.

Watkins: What I'm saying is that you absorb your poetry into your emotion, if we can distinguish, rather than putting your emotion into a poetic form. In the process you are controlled by emotion.

Manley: The poem seeks its own form. Is that what you mean?

Watkins: It automatically assumes its own form so much that you almost don't know that it is assuming a form.

Manley: That's right. I have always felt that some of the most successful stuff I've ever done is very quick and almost unrevised.

Watkins: That's true in my scholarship, but how do you account for Robert Lowell's saying he spent a hundred hours on one stanza?

Manley: He must have hit a rough spot. In poetry or any kind of creative work the mind can put things together in amazing ways that we can't even comprehend. Disparate things are put together by the mind in such a way that it seems like a miracle. But that doesn't happen all the time. The mind can also mess things up. So what you get are some miracles occurring and some messes. What you do is try to keep the miracles and get rid of the messes.

Watkins: Or improve the messes.

Manley: That's right. You have to bring a critical intelligence to it. But you have to ride the horse. And the horse is letting your mind go the way it wants to go.

Watkins: The miracle about your art is that after fifty-two years of intellectual education you are *not* an intellectual as you write poetry. You are *not* aware of your learning. Your learning has become as much a second nature to you as your love for your father.

Manley: I hope so.

Watkins: To what extent is this a unique Manley father-son poem, and to what extent is it a universal father-son poem? It is unique in the images isn't it?

Manley: Yes. The idea of sending five dollars to this place and that.

Watkins: That's the image. But it is not unique in its meaning?

Manley: No, I don't think so.

Watkins: Would you say that almost every father and son, close or distant, have their dead letters?

Manley: Yes.

Watkins: And that following the death of the father, it is the horror and the *glory* of the son to discover those dead letters?

Manley: That's right. A lot of children discover that their father kept a mistress, and their mother knew about it. Children discover intimate things about their parents that can be very distressing. In this case I discovered something about my real inheritance, which is not money or stocks or bonds or property, but an attitude toward the world. Instead of *getting* something for my inheritance, I found I was called upon to *give*.

Retardation Center

There in that place where each one is different,
Strange as God made us, the blind and the deaf
Grope at the world, or hang in a hug forever.
Smiles and tears are ready as feet to run.
Floors and walls are there to bounce off,
And demons appear in the middle of day.
There are minds so deep, so sunk
In their bodies, the flesh folds over
And ingrows itself to a sort of laugh
Feeling food, its texture and smell.
This is the place where those end up
Who were born with their souls for a body.
They are what they are.

They Are What They Are

Watkins: Tell me about the origin of this poem.

Manley: "Retardation Center" is a poem about a place where my wife worked. She introduced me to an attitude toward retarded people that I had not known before.

Watkins: What had you thought about retardation before you encountered it?

Manley: I had always regarded it as strange, and I still do. I regarded it as something depressing. Carolyn worked at a school for profoundly retarded people, people who were not only slow but who had multiple handicaps. Some were blind and deaf and retarded. They had almost no contact with the outer world. The attendants were trying to deal with these people in a minimal way, to train them to take care of themselves physically, not ever expecting to make them able to support themselves. They were trying to teach them how to brush their teeth and how to say a few words—just to do a few things. A nun began this school, and she found that because of her faith she could help these children in ways that people thought were not possible. She just believed they could be helped, and they were helped. Instead of warehousing them, stacking them up in an institution, she was trying to allow them to live at home in a family situation as long as possible. People thought these were absolutely hopeless cases, but some of them actually went on to school and received some minimal training. The nun would have been discouraged unless she had faith. She wouldn't have given them love and care. My wife worked at this school for maybe a year and kept wanting me to visit. She said it was such a wonderful place where wonderful things happened. I thought it would be very depressing.

Watkins: My reaction to the old, weak, dying, even close relatives and the retarded is that they are repulsive. Did you have that?

Manley: That's what I was afraid of. I kept saying I really did not want to go. I did not want to be upset, and my wife kept asking me to come anyway and saying that I would not be upset.

Watkins: Were you upset?

Manley: No.

Watkins: I still believe I would be. You think that's because I haven't been?

Manley: I think so. You haven't been with someone who has developed the attitude I learned from Carolyn. When I finally went, she showed me that you can look at it a different way. It isn't disgusting, repulsive, depressing. What you do is regard them as a different kind of human being. You just see their humanness and the hard work they put into the small gains they make. Carolyn could see something wonderful about their lack of a facade, their lack of a social mask. That's what I try to say in the poem: they are what they are. They do not know they are retarded. They don't hide behind disguises, like the rest of us do. Whatever they are, it's right out front. The rest of us have masks where we hide the deformities in ourselves.

Watkins: So they are not only retarded, but they have a kind of ultrahuman social genius?

Manley: It's a kind of innocence, a kind of goodness. They are *exactly* what you think they are. Where we may be really strange inside, we look normal outside.

Watkins: Is each kind of retardation different from every other kind?

Manley: Yes, each one is different, but they all share certain attributes. I'm trying to describe retardation and also to suggest something about the rest of mankind. The rest of mankind also has this deformed nature.

Watkins: Right.

Manley: The rest of mankind hides it, covers it up.

Watkins: Is the mask *our* retardation?

Manley: It's part of our handicap. I think that's the word for it; we're all handicapped, I'm trying to say. We cover it up. They have it out front.

Watkins: Since our handicaps are willful, they may not show as much, but they are worse.

Manley: Yes. You know, these people aren't malicious and cruel to one another.

Watkins: When you say that "the deaf grope at the world," have I caught you in a mixed figure, or are you saying their seeking for sound is a groping?

Manley: That's what I was thinking of. The sound isn't quite coming in, and therefore in a sense they're straining for it in the same way we grope in darkness.

Watkins: What is "hanging in a hug"? Hugging oneself?

Manley: I was thinking more that they were hugging one another.

Watkins: Then what is the hanging? They hang together as they hug?

Manley: They hang together. That way they aren't groping. They've already got hold of something.

Watkins: I was thinking not necessarily of the strait jacket, but of one so much retarded and within himself, he closes his arms and his eyes and hangs within himself, hugging himself.

Manley: That's a wonderful way to look at the line. It's not what I had in mind, but I think it would certainly be there in the words.

Watkins: That is to say, you are pleased to have in the poem the concept of the complete outgoingness of hanging together and also the ambivalence of the complete innerness of hugging oneself.

Manley: Yes. And I'm also pleased to see in the poem something I didn't know was there. Even if it's two people who are hanging together in a hug, it isn't as though they're in contact with the world. They're just in contact with another human being.

Watkins: Now is this a random bumping together or is this a deliberate *going* together and a feeling of love?

Manley: Well, I don't know. It doesn't really say what it is. I had the blind and the deaf groping, trying to come into contact with something, and then I had the next line "hanging in a hug."

Watkins: But it's not what *"it"* says; it's what the author says, isn't it?

Manley: I don't have a definite memory of what I intended when I wrote it, and I'm not certain it would be all that important even if I had.

Watkins: One thing I hope we both are saying about poetry is that there is a great deal of effort required for poetry, but once one makes the effort, he is bound to hit a lot of lucky things. They're not God-given, but they're not artistic accomplishments, just lucky successes.

Manley: I think what happens is that you arrange words and meanings and things on a page, and once you've made that arrangement, then they have a life of their own. At that point you have no more control over them. You've fixed them on the page; they're there in whatever relationship they have; and you can see many of the relationships because you put them there, but you don't see all of them. In this specific instance I was thinking that two individuals, groping around looking for some contact in the world, come on one another and then hang in there. *You* saw a different image, of one individual hugging himself. And I think that works perfectly.

Watkins: But the whole ambivalence is not in my reading, not in your reading, at this time, as reader, and not in your composition, but the luck of it comes from the complexity of retardation and of life.

Manley: I guess you could call it the "luck" of it. I don't know whether I'd call it the luck of it, because I don't think it's necessarily "lucky." This is basic to what happens when you create something.

Watkins: I think it is a *happening*, if you want to call it that instead of luck, but it is a happening because of the complexities of life as embodied in the figures. You write "Floors and walls are there" to indicate from the perspective of the retarded. No carpenter, no authority put them there, and therefore your "are there" gives the reader the surprise that the retarded person had when he hit them and bounced off.

Manley: That line is presented more from the point of view of the retardates themselves.

Watkins: And "demons appear in the middle of the day" is still their point of view?

Manley: I don't know now. At that point I could mean either the retardates themselves or the demons. Could go either way.

Watkins: Oh. Demons appear to the retarded, or the retarded are demons. How does that correspond with all your admiration of the retarded?

Manley: Well, it's mixed, Floyd. I think that I feel pity for them, and I think they can be demonic.

Watkins: As well as innocent.

Manley: Right. But what I was thinking of when I wrote the line was that they look like drawings of demons. They're deformed and distorted, demonic and crazy looking.

Watkins: Why do you have "in the middle of the day"?

Manley: I was working on Thomas More and his *Dialogue of Comfort*. Over half of the book is a meditation on the 91st Psalm and the temptation of the noon-day devil. It always seemed to me a very striking, strange image in the Psalm that the devil could appear in the middle of the day.

Watkins: Because it's not the time for devils.

Manley: That's right. They are there in broad daylight.

Watkins: The line is very effective to me, but I knew nothing whatsoever of Thomas More, and at the time of the composition of the poem you had More very much in mind.

Manley: I had him in mind, but I didn't expect anyone else to catch the allusion. What I wanted was the idea that you could see these demonic forces, not hidden at night in darkness, but in ordinary, normal daylight. There they are—among us.

Watkins: In the next passage, you have "the minds so deep, so sunk / In their bodies, the flesh folds over / And ingrows itself to a sort of . . ." I would have expected "sore" or "wound" or anything but laugh.

Manley: It's a strange line.

Watkins: The consequences are not those of the cause. What did you want with "laugh"?

Manley: I wanted "laugh" to be the thing that comes out of this kind of mind that's been buried in the flesh.

Watkins: Is it an admirable laugh that suddenly does see the light and is wonderful to the person, or is it an ironic laugh that one should laugh over what has been a horror?

Manley: The laugh is coming out of the retardate himself; he's laughing and laughing joyfully. This is a description of a retardate mind: that it is simply a laugh; it's so buried, so physical, that it becomes only a laugh as he feels food and its texture. He enjoys it and so he laughs.

Watkins: So, "he laughs" is a true enjoyment, and the irony comes from the fact that there should be this great surprise and great joy that is unexpected and aroused in the retardate by such a commonplace thing.

Manley: Not only that, but a person shouldn't be feeling his food. He's putting it to the wrong use. I wanted an outlandish image that would get to a really valid description of what this mental process is like. My daughter Mary worked last summer at a place in Florida, run by the state, for people with Downs' Syndrome. She told me an interesting story. One night the residents staged a rebellion. They didn't want to go to bed, and they kept saying, "No way, shitface!" And when she'd say, "Let's go to bed now," they all sat there and said, "No way, shitface!" and then they'd laugh and laugh and laugh. They all stayed up till about three in the morning, all yelling, "No way, shitface!" Finally they got into bed. (Laughing.) That's a touching story to me. Carolyn says mongoloid children are the most lovable children you will ever find in your life. She says she would much rather be with a mongoloid child than with a regular, normal child. She says they're much nicer in every respect.

But to get back to this image—what I was trying to do was to get some sense of the physical nature of a retarded person's mental processes. And so I took their mind, and I tried to bury it in their bodies. And then I tried to show a mental process occurring that was very physical—the kind of laughter that comes out of feeling food.

Watkins: What do you mean with the line "Who were born with their souls for a body." That to me is perhaps the most puzzling line in the poem.

Manley: It's really a repetition of the line "they are what they are." It probably suggests more than I can say, like most images do.

Watkins: And what does "they are what they are" mean?

Manley: What I intended is that unlike us, who disguise ourselves, they are truly whatever they are.

Watkins: So when we look at them, we see their souls instead of their bodies.

Manley: That's right. We see what they're really like. And we have souls that are deformed.

Watkins: We have a body, but the soul is not visible.

Manley: Yes. But with them their souls and bodies are the same thing. We have a kind of intelligence that gets in the way. I'm trying to articulate some things that are inarticulate for me, but what I'm saying in the poem is that our souls are very simple things, our bodies are very simple things, and our intelligence is very complicated.

Watkins: Does the line suggest also that they are much less aware than the usual person that they have a body? Unless some handicap intrudes itself to make something impossible or painful, they exist as minds without bodies.

Manley: Or souls without bodies. Or souls that are bodies. The fact that they are retarded means that their minds have partly gone away. It's very dim. I'm trying to suggest that their minds to them have become physical processes. They don't have the kind of cultural sophistication to disguise themselves. And therefore they are simpler beings and perhaps more pleasing to God, as many cultures think of retardates.

Watkins: Note: "Who were born with their souls for a body." Those who look at them see the body and not the soul.

Manley: I see what you're saying. Despite their multiple handicaps I was trying to praise them for something, a kind of innocence, a childishness, a lack of social sophistication that I found good. This poem started off to be a much longer poem. In fact, this was the first part, the introduction to a much longer poem about applesauce and about how they fed a girl applesauce to get her to walk.

Watkins: I'm not sure that I agree with you on this as being one of my favorite poems of those you have written. Let me tell you why.

Manley: Yes.

Watkins: I'm not sure you can distinguish between your experience and the poem. And that experience may be affecting you, and you may be reading that into the poem.

Manley: Could be.

Watkins: The poem has a problem. It has to convey to us what it conveys, through images that we cannot know, and therefore the images don't have the exactness that your images have in the poem about Erasmus.

Manley: I think they do.

Watkins: They have to be mysterious images because the minds of the retarded must remain so mysterious to us. So if the poem is to succeed it must succeed not through exact imagery but through mysterious imagery.

Manley: Well, there is a certain abstract quality. Now, that's true. I don't speak of any specific person. I speak of floors, and walls and demons and minds.

Watkins: And you don't speak of any particular look of the deformed, either. Nobody's slobbering. You know Faulkner writes the entire book about Benjy, and you never see him, and he is so lovable from the inside. In part 4 a great big hulking slobbering man with dead hair and dead eyes comes in, and he is terribly repulsive, and suddenly you realize that this is the person you loved all through the first book in *The Sound and the Fury*. That is an analogy to the insideness and outsideness of retardation.

Manley: Right. But, of course, there's really no comparison to what I'm trying to do here. What I'm trying to do is something very quick and brief.

Watkins: There's no parallel in the art form, but there is a parallel in the treatment of the same kind of mind.

Manley: Well, I'm trying to do something different still, I think. I'm not trying to get into the mind of a retardate in the same way Faulkner is. I'm trying to allow an observer to look at retardates and see them in a different way.

Watkins: Then at the same time, without a conscious awareness of it, you did get into their minds.

Manley: But only briefly. I was surprised to discover that I had at all; I think it's very oblique and very minor.

Watkins: I think it's very important that you do get slightly inside the mind of the retarded, so that I can feel more from outside the mind of the retarded.

Manley: We have to have a certain amount of sympathy for them, but I mean, for instance, "Floors and walls are there to bounce off" can be read not in terms of the point of view of the retardate, but simply that that's what they do with the floors and walls—they just bounce off them.

Watkins: I think once you have put retarded and nonretarded together, you have already confronted the "outside/inside" situation. I think you would be terribly crass if you hadn't got to some of the inside.

Manley: You have to have a measure of sympathy; that's what the poem is about really—sympathizing and regarding these people as people.

Watkins: And you can't have sympathy without being inside them.

Manley: No, that's right. But that's not what the poem is about. It's supposed to be dealing with our way of looking at them and seeing them as a metaphor for us. This poem uses their handicap to suggest something about people in society.

Watkins: Then the main thing is not about the retarded, but the main thing is that through seeing the retarded, we can realize how being unretarded we are so handicapped with a facade.

Manley: That's right. And what do our souls look like? If this is what their souls look like, what do our souls look like?

Watkins: So the poem is about the world of people who are not at the retardation center, and that's more important than those who are there?

Manley: I think so. I think they become a metaphor for us. It becomes a way of looking at both places.

Watkins: I would not say metaphor, but tool. They become a tool through which we may see ourselves.

Manley: A mirror. And you know the title "Retardation Center" suggests both, too.

Watkins: In what way?

Manley: Well, it suggests that we think of this as the retardation center, here, where we put all the retardates. And the whole world can be regarded as that, too.

Watkins: Then, being moral, *all* of us are in our retarded state.

Manley: Right. All of us are retarded.

Fig Bush

Master, look! The fig bush you cursed is dried up
—Mark 11:21

Beside the light wood of the wall
Where the sun sat under the leaves
Like an old man in a Victorian garden,
I planted the fig bush,
Exotic as Priapus this far north,
And waited for the fruit to swell like testicles.

And every winter the fig bush I planted
Withered from my thirtieth year,
Thin as the bodies of a paralyzed man
With a devil in him,
Touched by the weather
And died to the ground.

And every spring it started again,
The sparse, thin growth of the risen plant
Spreading like lust,
The strange leaves unfolding,
But bore no fruit.
Surely it's cursed.

The cold air dazzles.
The years inside me unfold.

Impotence and Dying

Watkins: Did this poem begin with a fig tree you planted, or with reading the Bible?

Manley: With a fig tree I planted.

Watkins: And did it get killed every year?

Manley: Every year. For a number of years. Finally it got to a good size and then it quit being killed as often, but it would freeze occasionally. My wife's grandfather had a lot of those old brown turkey figs, and I dug up one of them and replanted it.

Watkins: What's a turkey fig?

Manley: They call it "brown turkey." It's a shade of brown. He had a brown fig and a lemon colored fig.

Watkins: Why introduce the poem with a Biblical epigraph?

Manley: When I saw the fig tree dying every year, I thought of that verse in the Bible.

Watkins: Did you go back and read the Bible?

Manley: I'm sure I did. There are two references to the fig bush.

Watkins: I don't remember what the passage in the Bible meant. Do you?

Manley: No. The disciples walked by the fig bush that Christ had cursed; it had dried up, and they said, "Master, look, the fig bush you cursed has dried up."

Watkins: Doesn't it seem rather stupid to curse the fig tree?

Manley: Yes.

Watkins: Am I being blasphemous when I say that?

Manley: No. Let's look up Mark 11:21.

Watkins: All right.

Manley: This is the King James Version.

Watkins: A good Catholic like you are. (Laughter from both.)

Manley: Mark 11:21: "And Peter calling to remembrance saith unto him, Master, behold, the fig tree which thou cursedst is withered away. And Jesus answering saith unto them, Have faith in God. For verily I say unto you, That whosoever shall say unto this mountain, Be thou removed, and be thou cast into the sea; and shall not doubt in his heart, but believe that those things which he saith shall come to pass; he shall have whatsoever he saith." This is obviously a reference to a previous account of the fig tree.

Watkins: So he cursed the fruit tree as representative of unfruitful things. Is that right?

Manley: Yes. Here it is. "And on the morrow, when they were come from Bethany, he was hungry: And seeing a fig tree afar off having leaves, he came, if haply he might find any thing thereon: and when he came to it, he found nothing but leaves; for the time of figs was not yet. And Jesus answered and said unto it, No man eat fruit of thee hereafter for ever. And his disciples heard it." And then the next day: "And in the morning, as they passed by, they saw the fig tree dried up from the roots." And then Peter says, "Behold, the fig tree which thou cursedst is withered away."

Watkins: You have a vivid comparison in your poem. "Exotic as Priapus this far north," and Priapus was known for having a perpetual erection, was he not?

Manley: He was the god of gardens and fertility. That was his sign. (Laughs.) That was his sign.

Watkins: You intend that to be connected with the idea of the fruit swelling like testicles?

Manley: I wanted to develop a sexual metaphor. A minor one, running through the thing.

Watkins: Not a thematic one, but a sexual one?

Manley: It's a thematic metaphor, and it's a sexual metaphor. It picks up again in the word *lust* in the next to the last stanza.

Watkins: I see. What is the purpose of the sexual metaphor?

Manley: I want the fig bush to suggest something about personal power. It's used as a metaphor for personal powerfulness, I think, and so is the idea of sex. That is, the subject is not sex. Sex is a metaphor. Like the fig bush's bearing fruit: unfruitfulness. Impotence. But not sexual impotence. More spiritual impotence.

Watkins: Right. You say that you planted this fig bush in your thirtieth year. Is that poetical, agricultural, or both, or do they coincide?

Manley: I planted it sometime in my thirties. I was older than thirty.

Watkins: You wanted the thirtieth, poetically, for a reason other than metrics?

Manley: Yes. I wanted it because for some people I've heard the thirtieth year is a big turning point in their lives.

Watkins: A falling-off of sexual prowess?

Manley: No. The realization of age. The realization of loss of powers. Not sexual. But just a loss of powers—a sense of loss. Albert Camus said the thirtieth year is when you first become aware of time, and I had something like that in mind.

Watkins: Well, I think you do it with every decade or every few years. It's a perpetual condition.

Manley: Yes.

Watkins: I think that's a marvelous simile, "thin as the bones of a paralyzed man/ With a devil in him." Do you believe in devils, Frank?

Manley: No. I was remembering Christ healing paralytics and casting out demons.

Watkins: I asked you if you believed in devils. Do you believe in the devil?

Manley: No.

Watkins: I do.

Manley: I don't believe in devils. I don't believe in *the* devil. I believe in evil. I believe evil exists in people, but I don't think people are agents for a demonic force in the universe.

Watkins: I think they may put themselves in such a condition that they create demons within themselves.

Manley: All right, now I can believe that. Yes.

Watkins: And become demonic.

Manley: I can believe they can become demonic. I believe in evil, and I believe in evil's existence in people. But I don't believe in spiritual forces who are themselves evil.

Watkins: Does the Biblical epigraph relate to the devil?

Manley: Yes. I was thinking of a miracle by Jesus in one case and Jesus' cursing the fig bush in the other. He cures a paralyzed man and casts out the devil. In the case of the fig bush, he curses him.

Watkins: And yet both deal with fruitfulness and the lack of fruitfulness, or vigor and the lack of vigor, do they not?

Manley: That's right. What I was trying to suggest, Floyd, is the idea that some things are not in our control. That God chooses or not chooses according to his own ways.

Watkins: You have a vivid image in the fruit that swells like testicles. That, of course, is the shape of the fruit. But it's more than that also?

Manley: A couple of things come to mind. One is that they really do look like testicles. The color and the veining within the fig. The other thing is the image of fruitfulness. The fruitful metaphor and the sexual metaphor come together in the word *testicle*.

Watkins: In the Bible, hasn't the meaning so triumphed over image and practicality that the form in the Bible is almost altogether a parable?

Manley: I guess so. It's a strange story. It always seemed to me a strange story that Jesus would get angry at this fig tree because it wasn't in season. He wanted his food; he wanted a fig.

Watkins: How do you know it wasn't in season?

Manley: It said that. It said that it wasn't in season; it was not the time for figs.

Watkins: Does that mean it was not the time for figs, or does it mean that this fig tree was in the time for figs but it wasn't figging?

Manley: Well, I took it to mean that it wasn't the time for figs. And Jesus got angry.

Watkins: Now that makes the purpose of the passage in the Bible so much parable and meaning that it almost makes the story, except for parable and meaning, incomprehensible, or at least extremely puzzling, doesn't it?

Manley: *Very* puzzling. What it says is "for the time of figs was not yet." So it sounds like the tree had leaves on it, but "the time of figs was not yet," and Jesus got angry with it because it was not bearing figs when it was not the season for it. What interested me about the story, now that I think about it, was the incomprehensibility. I was thinking of Jesus' cursing the fig bush as being similar to the weather's killing it.

Watkins: I see. The weather is killing it as it does in north Georgia and as the fig tree is an inappropriate plant for weather as cold as the winter is in north Georgia.

Manley: I was thinking of the processes of weather as like God's decision.

Watkins: Do you think of your poem as a parable?

Manley: I never thought of it as that. But I guess you're right: it does have a parable.

Watkins: According to modern tastes, aren't parables in poetry a little bit excessively allegorical?

Manley: Right. I guess that's why I hesitated a little bit when you asked me that. I thought of it not as a parable, but as a metaphor. I was developing a couple of metaphors.

Watkins: Now that you do think of it, which do you think it is, metaphor or parable?

Manley: I think it's metaphor, because the Biblical parable is not entirely clear to me.

Watkins: Then our poem is clearer than the Bible?

Manley: No, the parable in the Bible is not clear to me, and my poem is not too clear to me.

Watkins: Your poem is not clear to you?

Manley: No.

Watkins: Where does the mystery come from—the Bible or the condition of unfruitfulness or the climate?

Manley: Well, I don't know what attitude I have toward the weather, toward God's control of the weather. I don't know what I'm saying about this relationship between the bones of a paralyzed man with the devil in him. I don't know what relationship that has to the fig bush.

Watkins: So the poet may write things which are mysterious to him and which he has not figured out at the time of writing.

Manley: Yes. He does not take the time to figure them out. They just seem to go all right.

Watkins: Did you deliberately think that you intended to give great emphasis to the last two lines by setting them apart in a shorter stanza?

Manley: Yes.

Watkins: Then what do you mean by "the cold air dazzles"? What is the cold air and whom does it dazzle?

Manley: In the last two lines the application is made to the person. The poem at that point becomes metaphor.

Watkins: To the person—the persona or the poet?

Manley: The persona/poet.

Watkins: You would not distinguish between the two?

Manley: Well, I'm speaking about myself in part here.

Watkins: Yourself and other men as they are in you also.

Manley: Right.

Watkins: What does "the cold air dazzle" then? The cold air dazzles all men?

Manley: Yes. I think so.

Watkins: All men. And then, so, what is the cold air that does dazzle all men? Thirty years? Forty years?

Manley: (Laughs.) Yes. That same process. The poem wonders why what happens to people happens to them. Why does God do the things He does?

Watkins: Is it that we are planted outside of our climate?

Manley: I don't know. That could be. Maybe we're in the wrong place or time. It could be just the process of age and time. Like the seasons. One season yields to another. It may be that we flourish in summer and die in winter.

Watkins: And then are not reborn, at least in this world, in the spring?

Manley: Right. What I'm trying to do here is suggest that the "cold air dazzles" is like winter to the fig bush, and that the years inside me are unfolding like leaves of a fig bush. And that there is this process of annual death.

Watkins: Do we unfold at the moment of birth of the leaf, or at the moment of death?

Manley: I thought of the annual resurrection of the fig bush. Each winter it's killed. Each year it comes back again, always striving to produce fruit but never making it.

Watkins: So the poem really ends on a very strong note of optimism. Even though you and the fig tree are going to have to die again, the poem ends with the leaves of the fig tree unfolding, ready to be cursed again.

Manley: Right. A curious kind of optimism: nothing's going to happen, but it will keep trying.

Watkins: That's rather strange when you also say "the years unfold," referring to the aging process.

Manley: That's part of it, too, I think.

Watkins: So this last line is really a knotty paradox.

Manley: It goes a lot of different ways at once. The two main ways are the resurrection in spring as the leaves come back to the bush and the aging process, the years within the individual. It's a poem about impotence and about dying.

Watkins: Impotence and dying. And one is likely to remind you of the other.

Manley: Yes. Death does not allow people to fulfill themselves. The aging process, the time that we're caught in, the winter of our years, does not allow us to fulfill ourselves. Everyone who has ever lived is disappointed. There's something about being alive that will lead you to some kind of disappointment somewhere along the line. I wasn't really doing anything more than just raising the question in my own mind: why is it people have this sense of potential in their lives and then a sense of loss of expectations?

Old Worlds

Poor Tom

I can understand the monkeys, Thomas,
And a weasel or two, some parrots in cages,
Maybe even a Barbary ape, a gift
From the Spanish ambassador for sevices rendered.
Good for the children. Part of the plan.
Not that Erasmus would ever approve.
St. Jerome's lion was more his style:
In a desert, where the sun bears down
As sharp as his mind without shadow.
Your beasts, Thomas, were caged in a garden,
Shaded by shrubs, behind the house.
Henry Patenson fed them, a natural,
Grinning and smacking his lips as they ate.
Dame Alice could hardly tell you apart.
And sometimes on Fridays—I understand, Thomas—
Leaving the shape of your life at the altar,
The heretics bound and lashed in your study,
You'd visit in private the king and his council,
The great lords at Lambeth, in cages,
God's creatures all—antic, amusing:
Weasel or monkey or parrot or ape.
You could hardly tell them apart,
You, the only free man among them.
I understand that. Hall said you joked
Your way to the scaffold: a matter of style.

But Cliff, Thomas—Cliff. What cage
Or cell did you keep him in
After you took him by the hand
And led him away from knocking the heads
Off statues of saints on the bridge to the Tower?
Where did he stay in the garden?
And what did you see in him, Thomas?
Compassion, perhaps, a work of mercy?
Or did you see yourself there at last?
The mad eyes innocent and full of anger,
Caged in himself: your own *momento mori*,
The head and the sharpened ax the same:
The outcast, the shape of your life at the altar?
Cliff waits in the cage, Thomas.
He cannot rest. He cannot be kept,
Cannot be loosed till the king claims
The garden and the cages all open.
Then Cliff roams free,
And your head returns to its place on the bridge.
Your distant eyes look down from the pike.
They do not see Cliff pass in the crowd.
He walks on the water, over the Thames,
Other things on his mind now,
Not heads, looking for something
To find in a storm, somewhere to rest,
Some hovel. Poor Tom,
Poor Turleygod, poor Tom.

Saint Thomas More and Other Martyrs

Watkins: You have said that your historical poems like "Poor Tom" are, in large part, inventions. What does that mean?

Manley: That I don't feel limited by history. I change it, add to it, invent it.

Watkins: It is immoral, false, unartistic, for a writer to alter history?

Manley: It would be for a historian. But I grant myself certain license.

Watkins: Why does an artist need license?

Manley: It's not a matter of need. It's a matter of desire. You want to do certain things, and you manipulate things to do them. History binds and limits.

Watkins: Is there any way of describing the nature of what you want when you invent?

Manley: In "Poor Tom" I want to understand something. I ask a lot of questions that I don't really get clear answers to.

Watkins: Answers from whom?

Manley: From the person I'm asking the questions of. I want to understand Thomas More. I ask him a lot of questions, and none of the answers come through very clearly. He is a saint because he was a martyr. He gave up his life for his faith. That interested me.

Watkins: Is that what made you write a poem about Thomas More?

Manley: Yes. I have been working on him in a scholarly way since about 1965.

Watkins: Seventeen years. How many books have you written about him?

Manley: One. And I'm finishing another now.

Watkins: Will this be the last one?

Manley: God willing.

Watkins: What are they?

Manley: One is the *Dialogue of Comfort*, which More wrote as a prisoner in the Tower of London just before he was executed. He wrote the book in order to prepare himself to die. I edited it with Louis L. Martz for the Yale edition of More's *Complete Works*. I dealt mostly with the intellectual history. If More said, "Ambrose saith," for example, I went and found out where Ambrose said it. Then I wrote a good part of the lengthy introduction to the book. I also did a modernized text edition that's out in paperback. Right now I'm translating one of More's Latin works for the Yale edition—one of his polemical works against Luther.

Watkins: When did you decide to write "Poor Tom"?

Manley: After I finished editing the book More wrote in the Tower.

Watkins: Do you remember an immediate impetus that made you say, "Oh, I'll write "Poor Tom' "?

Manley: No. But I remember when I wrote it. One afternoon I had been swimming. Then I went to my carrell in the library, sat down, and wrote a draft of it. The questions it raises were on my mind. What I'm trying to understand in this poem is a man who had many things given him in the world—who was wealthy, who had a loving family, who had position, prestige, fame, respect. I'm trying to understand why he gave all that up and chose to die.

Watkins: Besides your puzzlement, did you also have a feeling of contempt or admiration?

Manley: Oh, admiration. But also puzzlement. More chose to become an outcast. He could have stayed in his society. He could have remained a member in good standing. What he chose instead was to become like a derelict on skid row, a person who was abandoned, cast out. This puzzled me a great deal.

Watkins: Cast out, but not drunk.

Manley: No. No. Not drunk. Cast out, thrown in prison, neglected, all his money taken away from him, his family impoverished, threatened with physical torture and death.

Watkins: Is that puzzlement revealed in your scholarship as well as in the poetry?

Manley: Oh, yes. That's what I was trying to deal with in the book I was working on.

Watkins: Where have you reached a better answer?

Manley: In the poem, I think.

Watkins: You couldn't put it in the scholarship because that would have meant too much conjecture? You can conjecture in the poem, create, but you could not in the scholarship?

Manley: I could carry more emotion to it in the poem than I could in the scholarship. The problem for the author is in trying to put something in clear, unmistakable terms when the material itself is murky, not clear, not unambiguous.

Watkins: What is the source of the monkeys, the weasel, the parrots, the ape?

Manley: The literal source is the zoo More had. He was interested in animals and in educating his children; so he kept a kind of zoo in his house. He collected animals and he enjoyed watching them. I meant two things by the animals. I was referring, of course, to animals as being the things in us that are chained up, too. Our animal natures.

Watkins: Then the zoo reflects the animal nature of Saint Thomas More?

Manley: I meant that to be an overtone, but I wanted to talk literally about the animals themselves in their cages back in the garden. More had an estate outside London, and he kept his beasts there.

Watkins: What is the meaning of "part of the plan"?

Manley: More spent a good bit of time seeing to the education of his children. Their teachers became friends and important members of his household.

Watkins: Did he want to teach his children about their own animality?

Manley: No, just about animals. People in the Renaissance were curious about exotic animals. De Busbecq, for example, the emperor's ambassador to the Turks, heard about a giraffe that had just died in Istanbul two weeks before he got there; so he and some friends dug it up to examine its bones. They called it a cameleopard.

Watkins: Who was Erasmus?

Manley: A famous scholar and friend of More's who visited him often and spent time in his house.

Watkins: From another poem you have written about Erasmus I would think you might regard him as incapable of anything beyond a kind of intellectual friendship.

Manley: Well, More apparently had a genius for friendship. I don't know about Erasmus.

Watkins: In the poem what would Erasmus not have approved of?

Manley: Keeping animals. He was interested in high-powered scholarship—Jerome and commentaries on the Vulgate, editions of the New Testament, and things like that.

Watkins: Is St. Jerome's lion in the poem a living or a sculptured lion?

Manley: I was thinking of a picture I've seen of St. Jerome. It shows him with a lion. He's translating the Bible into Latin, and he has a lion out in the desert with him.

Watkins: Would Erasmus have approved of that lion?

Manley: He would have approved of that one because it's an allegorical lion.

Watkins: Approve of lions so long as they aren't real lions.

Manley: So long as they're not real animals, just scholarly and iconographical.

Watkins: Are you struggling with the spirit and animalism of man in the way Sir Thomas More did?

Manley: The poem moves on. The next stanza moves toward what I cannot understand. More kept not only animals, but people too. The thing he's aiming for is to understand other natures, human beings and animals too.

Watkins: Explain the simile "as sharp as his mind without shadow."

Manley: That line describes Erasmus: his mind was sharp. There were no shadows in his mind—just intellect, like the sun bearing down on a desert—all rational, no murkiness, no shadowiness, no bestiality to Erasmus, as there may have been to More.

Watkins: So St. Thomas More's mind contains shadows, and Erasmus's does not; and having the shadow of the complexity of life is really paradoxically much more human and lovable to you than having a mind without a shadow?

Manley: Right. It seemed to me that Erasmus was inhuman to the degree that he was just an intellect in a vacuum, just rationality only.

Watkins: Who was "Henry"?

Manley: More's fool, Henry Patenson. He was a step up from the beast. He was a moron.

Watkins: Are you going up a ladder of human beings from the beginning of the poem to the end?

Manley: Yes. People in the Renaissance kept morons in their houses and used them as fools. It seems cruel to us, but they were amused by them. If you look at Holbein's portrait of More's family, the most handsome man in the entire picture is Henry Patenson. More was interested in the absurd things he would have to say about things.

Watkins: You don't find compassion in More for Patenson?

Manley: I think there was compassion. He treated him like one of his children, but he was a man More's age. More tells a story about a time when he went on an embassy to the continent and took Henry Patenson with him. At an important state dinner, Henry Patenson was sitting with the others, and some of the foreigners started teasing him and throwing pieces of bread at him. Henry Patenson became very angry. He stood up and said in English, "Anyone who throws any more bread at me, I'm going to hit them with something." The foreigners did not understand English; so they kept on throwing food at him, and he finally hit them with rocks. More thought it amusing that Henry Patenson didn't understand enough to know that not everyone speaks English. (Laughs.)

Watkins: Did he think it was amusing that some people were hit with rocks?

Manley: I think he thought it was probably an interesting interruption to a state dinner.

Watkins: What's the derivation of *natural* as meaning "moron"?

Manley: I don't know. I think it means a natural man—one who is uncultured, uncivilized, as opposed to social man.

Watkins: Patenson fed the animals as a sort of servant?

Manley: That's my invention: That one of his chores was to feed the animals.

Watkins: "Grinning and smacking his lips as they ate." Is that the moron's vicarious enjoyment of imagining he is eating with the animals?

Manley: Yes. He eats in sympathy; he moves his lips.

Watkins: Like a dentist who holds his mouth a certain way as he drills.

Manley: The more we talk about this, the more I realize that it really is a very private poem. It derives from the great amount of time I've spent with the subject. People can't be expected to know much about Henry Patenson.

Watkins: Is that a weakness, a deliberate obscurantism?

Manley: That's not the poet's problem. I wanted to make a statement that was meaningful to me. A poet writes these things for himself and hopes that other people will be interested.

Watkins: Now let's meet another stranger. Who is Dame Alice?

Manley: (Laughs.) I go back now into biography. Dame Alice was More's second wife, a most inappropriate wife for him. She was loud-spoken, opinionated, masculine, a woman with no intellectual pretensions whatsoever. She said exactly what she thought. Her husband in her opinion was a fool, particularly at the end when he wouldn't get out of prison. She could not comprehend his refusal. More joked with her and about her all the time. He handled her very well.

Watkins: Did he perhaps marry her as a person like Henry Patenson to have more fun with?

Manley: She was a member of the menagerie, yes. But More married her because he needed a wife for his children. He must have thought she would be a good one. She was a very loyal woman. She had many good traits and many bad traits, but she really thought her husband was an idiot. He would sit there drawing pictures in the ashes, she said, instead of getting out and making a name for himself.

Watkins: Are ashes your figure for ink?

Manley: No. He'd sit there with a stick and play around the fire. She thought he ought to be up and about and doing. That's why I say she could hardly tell St. Thomas More from Henry Patenson.

Watkins: Or the animals. And how would Thomas "leave the shape of his life at the altar"?

Manley: More had a lot of money, and he built a building on his estate that he called the New Building. Every Friday he stepped out of the world, he said. He went into the New Building and he spent the day in prayer and meditation. He literally spoke of it as stepping out of the world. He put down all his business and refused to receive any calls. He was just there. He spent his time mostly meditating and praying. I imagine a crucifix on the altar, and I imagine what happened to More at the end of his life as being similar to what happened to Christ.

He imitated Christ and walked the way of the cross.

Watkins: Now he is St. Thomas, and you respect him and admire him. Aren't you being a little too intimate with a saint when you call him just Tom?

Manley: Well, I feel intimate with him.

Watkins: You regard him as such a friend that you can call him Thomas or Tom and leave off the "Saint"?

Manley: Yes. At least in this poem.

Watkins: Who were the heretics?

Manley: Well, that's another side of More that's curious and fascinating. More was a man of powerful hatreds. You wouldn't expect it really; he seemed so flexible and easy a person—such a good sense of humor. A contradictory man. He really had powerful passions which came pouring out against the heretics, as he called them—the Protestants of the time. In the poem I imagine him binding them and lashing them—referring of course to books that are bound. He was writing about Luther and the other heretics, but he was also binding and lashing them in another sense. He was accused of sentencing a number of early English Protestants to be scourged. I don't know whether that's true or not. To understand what he did when he died you have to understand the kind of passion with which he treated issues like this. He felt very strongly about certain things and was willing to take very strong positions.

Watkins: What's Lambeth?

Manley: Lambeth Palace. That was where More was first interrogated.

Watkins: Were the great lords actually in cages or prisons?

Manley: No. I imagine that when More went out in his garden and looked at the animals he would see there reflections of Henry the Eighth and his council. (Laughs.) He would see various great men of state—the monkey in this cage, the fox in that, the weasel in another, and giraffe in another.

Watkins: So their cages were not prisons but were privy chambers or something of that sort?

Manley: Yes.

Watkins: Also, they were caged within the limitations of their own souls? In a way, the animals, the king and his council, and the moron and the lord are all linked together by implication in their limitations.

Manley: They're all caged in themselves, and the poem moves toward the idea that perhaps More was too. He was less caged, but I wonder whether he wasn't really caged in and couldn't help himself. Caged in by his own personality.

Watkins: How are all of these "God's creatures"?

Manley: I mean that ironically. I'm trying to push together the animals in the cages and the king and all the important people at court. They all are really under God. Animals seem to know by instinct that they're God's creatures, but kings often forget they are.

Watkins: How is St. Thomas More the only free man among them?

Manley: Well, in one sense, literally. As he walked among the animals, they were in cages and he was free. I imagined also that he was the only free man among the king and his council. He kept his distance, his integrity.

Watkins: He simply said, "I refuse." Now what about this line: "Hall said you joked your way to the scaffold." Who was Hall?

Manley: A contemporary historian and a very prejudiced man. He said that Thomas More was really a despicable person because even when he was dying he made jokes. And he thought this was unsuited to the seriousness of the occasion. I think it's a matter of real grace—grace under pressure. More grew a long beard in prison, and he said to the man who was going to chop his head off, "Don't chop my beard off; it had nothing to do with it." So he placed his beard out of the way of the ax. When he was climbing up on the scaffold, it was very shaky, and he said to the man who was going to kill him, "Help me up. As for coming down, I'll shift for myself." He knew he wasn't coming down under his own power. That sort of thing, Hall said, was indecorous. If you're going to be executed for treason, he thought, you shouldn't make jokes.

Watkins: You appreciate it as grace and, shall we say, saintliness under pressure?

Manley: Yes, I think it's amazing. It shows great courage and acceptance of one's death.

Watkins: How was More killed?

Manley: An executioner with a big ax chopped his head off.

Watkins: The head was chopped off on a scaffold?

Manley: Yes, to elevate the person so that the crowd could get a good view. It was a public spectacle.

Watkins: This next stanza suggests a great shift in the mind of the poet. Who is Cliff?

Manley: The first stanza is in a sense all the things I can understand. I can understand the animals. I can even understand someone making jokes when he's dying. What I *can't* understand is what comes next, and that is his choosing to die. The poem is moving now toward the reasons for his dying, for his choosing death. I begin with Cliff, a person More tells about in one of his polemical works. More's polemical works are usually very dull. They are arguments that were passionate at the time, but now have passed away from most people's concerns. They are mostly theological arguments. In the anecdote I have in mind More tells how a man named Cliff had been picked up by the authorities on London Bridge. At that time there were many statues on the bridge—the Virgin Mary in particular with the Baby in her arms. Cliff would go up to the statues and start arguing with them as if they were real people. Then he would get mad at them, hit them, and knock their heads off. So the authorities apprehended him and took him to More, who was a judge. They wanted More to put him in prison, but More took him into his own house instead. Cliff was obviously a madman.

Watkins: Did he have a last name?

Manley: No. He was referred to only as Cliff. Of course, no one knows whether Cliff really existed or whether More just made him up. There's no other reference to him in More's work except in this anecdote.

Watkins: That is a kind of characterization. The strange and the unusual or a slave might be known only by a first name.

Manley: Or a madman might have forgotten his last name. You ask him, "What's your name?" And he'd say, "Cliff." More says that's the way Protestants do. They go around and knock the heads off saints. So he may have made the whole thing up, inventing an anecdote. I chose to assume that Cliff really existed and really did go up to the statues and argue with them and knock their heads off.

Watkins: Why would More have said he might have existed if he didn't? As a parable?

Manley: Yes. In order to make his point: that Protestants reject the doctrine of saints. And so he imagines a madman going around knocking their heads off.

Watkins: Why do you ask what cage or cell Thomas kept Cliff in?

Manley: Because I assume More took him home and put him in his menagerie along with Henry Patenson, Dame Alice, and the animals. Cliff was mad, and I imagine he had to keep him in a cage or a padded cell. I wanted to make the point that he collected him too. He even collected Cliff.

Watkins: Yet More had sympathy toward Cliff as well as toward Henry Patenson?

Manley: Right.

Watkins: You write that Cliff was "caged in himself: your own *momento mori*, / The head and the sharpened ax the same: / The outcast, the shape of your life at the altar."

Manley: Here I'm moving toward the idea that in the eyes of the world at least More was crazy. He collected Cliff and took him home because he was being compassionate. That's my first thought. Then I wonder if More actually saw himself there at last. Did he find in Cliff something that reflected him or mirrored something in himself? If the animals reflected the king and his council, then does Cliff and his craziness reflect you? I ask More that. His mad eyes innocent and full of anger like yours? Caged in himself like you are? Your own *momento mori*—a reflection perhaps of how you will die, your own decapitation? That's what I was working toward. But this part of the poem gets very problematic. I'm moving toward what it was that made More do this apparently insane thing. I'm looking for an image for that, a way to represent it, and the image I find is Cliff.

Watkins: Then "Cliff roams free," I suppose, is literal—his enjoyable freedom following Thomas's death.

Manley: Yes. The thing that Cliff represents—the mad choice to die for one's principles—still goes on. If madness is something illogical, extraordinary, then there may be an edge of madness in More. Judging him from the point of view of the king and any powerful man of his time, the choice he made was mad. He impoverished his family; he killed himself. That's the point of similarity I want to point to—Cliff's knocking the heads off statues of saints on the bridge to the Tower and the image of More's own decapitation by his own choice: "The head and the sharpened ax the same." I'm pushing things together here, and I don't know whether they go together clearly or not.

Watkins: How is the line "the shape of your life at the altar" toward the end of the poem changed since the use of it in the middle of the first stanza?

Manley: That's a good question. It is almost the same thing, but the repetition picks up something else I think. The first reference was clearly to a crucifix. The second reference is to a Jewish tradition called the *anaw*. I ran into it when I was working on More. It's a reference to the man who is cast out of his society, who has his whole mode of life and all his possessions taken from him. Job was *anaw*—outcast—in this way. He was abandoned, made derelict like the people you see in our cities today who have been released from insane asylums and have no one to take care of them. Christ in his crucifixion claimed relationship with this tradition when he cried out with Jeremiah and Isaiah, "My God, my God, why hast thou forsaken me?" It is the cry of one who feels himself abandoned not only by those around him, but even by God. I imagine More to be a member of that same group—the *anaw*, the outcast, the abandoned, the derelict, whose only hope is to hope beyond hope.

Watkins: Why does Cliff walk on the water? Over the Thames.

Manley: I wanted to suggest that after More dies the thing that Cliff represents in him goes on.

Watkins: Then you are relating Cliff and Thomas More to the miracle of Christ's walking on the water?

Manley: I'm reflecting that. But I mean literally that Cliff walked over the bridge, over London Bridge and out into the countryside. He keeps going. What we admire in More is a kind of madness—if you view him from the eyes of society. I think we pick up the same kind of madness in a great number of people we admire.

Watkins: You pointed up your metaphor by using the word "on" the water instead of "over" the water.

Manley: Right.

Watkins: Finally, is Poor Tom saintly to you?

Manley: Yes, he is. I don't think you have to understand him fully to admire him. The poem is trying to point toward something about suffering too. People who suffer intensely pass on some hope to us. We don't have to do exactly what society tells us to. We can choose not to. I find it admirable that More suffered and suffered intensely for his convictions and yet did not give way or lose hope.

Watkins: Is his hope mortal, or is it for immortality?

Manley: Immortal. It was complicated and very difficult, but it was a belief in another life. More underwent great fear, great loss, during the year or so he was in prison, but he never gave way. He never lost his hope and trust in God. No matter what happened to his physical body, his soul remained his own possession.

Watkins: What does "Your head returns to its place on the bridge" mean?

Manley: That goes back to Cliff's knocking the heads off the statues of saints. Literally, of course, that's where More's head was placed after it was chopped off. They put it on a pike and exhibited it on London Bridge as all heads of traitors were exhibited. Then the bodies were left unburied.

Watkins: I do not find "Turleygod" in any of my usual dictionaries. What is it?

Manley: It's an allusion to *King Lear*. This poem is very private, and I'm not really concerned with whether the audience follows it or not. It refers to Act III, Scene 3, in *King Lear*, where Edgar disguises himself as a mad beggar. He goes around saying, "Poor Turleygod, Poor Tom."

Watkins: Did "Turley" have a common meaning as a noun?

Manley: I don't know. I always took *Turleygod* as one of Shakespeare's inventions. He has poor Tom speak all sorts of gibberish. What happens is that King Lear is driven out of the society he once ruled and sees himself reflected in Tom and learns some compassion and sympathy for others. There is more than a suggestion in the play that we are all fools and madmen who need to find shelter from the storm. When I used to teach at Yale, I remember I had to pass through the New Haven Common to get to my Shakespeare class. As I passed through the common, I could usually see a lot of alcoholics sleeping in the sun. They had their shoes tied around their necks so that no one would steal them. As I passed through the common and saw them there, I remember thinking that's what Shakespeare is talking about in *King Lear*—this quality of being outcast, like Job or Christ, of being abandoned, outside one's society and hopeless. That's really what I'm trying to get at in this poem. The consequences of that and the hope for all of us that rises mysteriously from it.

Heliogabalus

When the Emperor Heliogabalus
Was told by a Syrian oracle
That he would die a violent death,
He had a special noose prepared
Of woven blue and scarlet silk
And a Nubian slave to carry it by day
And sleep with it by his side at night
So that he could be garroted in imperial purple
By his own shadow.
And he had golden swords prepared,
Poisons from Egypt, conclusions infinite
Of easy ways to die
Coiled in the cunning hollow of a ring—
Carnelians, sapphires, emeralds, diamonds,
Carbuncles rounder than a woman's breast
Contrived to suck the blood asleep—
And in the courtyard built a tower
Higher than the topmost turrets of Rome,
The swirling grain of the scaffolding
Gilded in patterns of solid gold,
Steps inlaid with precious stone,
Jade and lapis lazuli,
And there he would run when death
Came after and fling himself off
So that all men forever would be struck dumb
At the wonder and the beauty and the glory of his going—
The elegance and mastery of Heliogabalus,
The last of the line of the Antononies.

But when the time came for his death
And Fate led the Praetorian Guard
To attack the palace and free the state,
They found the Emperor coiled like a snake
Inside the cunning hollow of a privy.
When he was killed, he fell in the pit.
They dug him out and lashed him to an axle
And dragged him through the squares of the city,
Through the dust of the track at the Circus.
Then they stuffed him in a sewer,
But he got stuck halfway in,
And they weighted him with stones instead
And threw him off the Aemilian Bridge
So no one could ever bury the body.
The soldiers who killed him spoke no Latin.
The Senate ordered his name erased
From public works and public record.
But the people remembered. They called him
Big Ass and Shit Face
And told the story from father to son
While the story held up.
And then they forgot him.

Except for some. They are the ones
Who are haunted in sleep by a freckled hand
That holds a severed head like a lantern
And a voice that says over and over:
                    The time is free.

The Art of Dying

Watkins: Are the facts of your poem imagined or taken from a source that you read about Heliogabalus?

Manley: Half and half, I guess.

Watkins: What was the source?

Manley: The *Scriptores Historiae Augustae*, the writers of the history of the caesars. These are short Latin biographies of late Roman emperors.

Watkins: When did Heliogabalus live? Late Roman?

Manley: Yes. And he was a kind of monster, a spiritual monster. He's often referred to as one of the most monstrous of the Roman emperors.

Watkins: Monstrous in violence?

Manley: Monstrous in cruelty, monstrous in expenditure. I remember John Donne refers to him in *The Anniversaries*, which is the first place I ran into him. Donne says Heliogabalus would do things like burning million-dollar bills. If he had a million dollar bill in his hand, he would set fire to it to see it burn. He didn't give a shit. Just burn it up. You know, that kind of madness, that kind of bizarre streak.

Watkins: What in your poetic imagination makes you associate yourself with such monsters?

Manley: (Laughs.) Well, I know they're interesting. (Pauses.) I don't associate myself with them. I was a classics major when I was an undergraduate and an English major. I continued Latin, and I do a lot of research in Latin. So this comes out of that area of my life. But this poem has led to a series of poems which I did last year on other Roman emperors. I did about twenty or thirty of them.

Watkins: Are they published?

Manley: Some of them are coming out in the *Sewanee*, and the whole volume is currently being submitted to publishers.

Watkins: You are not a great admirer of most Roman emperors?

Manley: No. No. In fact I have a quotation from St. Paul saying that these are the rulers of the world of shadows.

Watkins: Do you know of any modern poet who has written poems about Roman emperors?

Manley: No.

Watkins: Robert Penn Warren has two, one about Tiberius and one on Domitian. (Pauses.) What is a Syrian oracle, Frank?

Manley: Just a person from Syria, an oracle in Syria. I think that may have come from the life of Heliogabalus.

Watkins: Syria was in the Middle East?

Manley: Yes. Roughly where it is now.

Watkins: What is a garrot?

Manley: It's a thing to choke people with. Sometimes the Turkish emperors used a bowstring. It can be any kind of rope slung around the neck.

Watkins: The dictionary calls it Spanish. To my surprise.

Manley: Right.

Watkins: It defines it as an iron collar screwed tight with a knob. But you were thinking of a rope.

Manley: I was thinking of a rope, yes.

Watkins: Did Heliogabalus imagine that that would be the method? Or did the oracle tell him that?

Manley: No, the oracle told him that he would die a violent death. So he was making arrangements for it. The first arrangement he made was to have a slave go around with him carrying a special rope to do it with.

Watkins: And he would be wearing the imperial purple?

Manley: Yes. He would go down in his robe, as it were. Even the thing that choked him to death would be imperially prepared.

Watkins: "By his own shadow"—what does that mean?

Manley: That is the Nubian slave, the black man. He chose a black slave to go with him. When the black slave killed him, it would be like killing himself. He would give the command to the slave, and it was as though his own shadow killed him.

Watkins: Is this shadow metaphorical as well as human?

Manley: Yes.

Watkins: That is, the shadow of death hovering near him is that slave going along with him?

Manley: Right. I can't remember whether I made that up or whether that was part of the story.

Watkins: Why does he wish to die in purple? What difference does it make what you die in?

Manley: That's the whole point. He wants to go out in splendor and glory. He wants to die in a way that's appropriate for an emperor. He doesn't want to die with just a white cord slung around his neck choking him to death. It has to be imperial purple. So he has a special one prepared.

Watkins: So he wants to go out himself like the million dollar bill.

Manley: Right. He wants to be perfect. He's going to arrange his death. He has gone to the oracle. The oracle has told him it's going to happen. And so now he's preparing it to be really splendid.

Watkins: You report no emotional reaction on his part to the prophecy.

Manley: That's right.

Watkins: You wished the images to convey that in the poetry entirely.

Manley: Right.

Watkins: Was there any reported emotional reaction to the prophecy in the sources?

Manley: No. The sources are very poorly done. They don't really get into the personalities. They just report facts. They are poor historians. They are chroniclers.

Watkins: Factual chroniclers. (Pauses.) Is Antonines the name of his royal house?

Manley: Right. His royal house. He is the last of them.

Watkins: Did you have any other great figure in mind?

Manley: I remember as I was writing it references to Shakespeare's *Antony and Cleopatra* crept in. "Conclusions infinite of easy ways to die." I think that's almost straight Shakespeare. Cleopatra was rumored to have sought easy ways to die.

Watkins: Was the asp an easy way?

Manley: That's right. The asp was an easy way.

Watkins: It was painless death, though it was a snake?

Manley: In the line here, "Contrived to suck the blood asleep," I was thinking of the asp. Cleopatra says, "It sucks me to sleep," as she puts the asp to her breast. It sucks its victim to sleep, so that the lines, "Carbuncles rounder than a woman's breast/ Contrived to suck the blood asleep" is a combination of Cleopatra and the idea of a carbuncle as being a rounded jewel. I was trying to think of splendid things. I wanted the imagery to be very opulent and wealthy, very rich, very imperial.

Watkins: Did you use the play in other ways?

Manley: I just noticed it. "Higher than the topmost turrets of Rome." That's a reference, I think, to Helen of Troy. I don't know why I kept thinking about women in this.

Watkins: (Chuckles.) Maybe because you do a lot of the time.

Manley: (Laughs.) Maybe. "Was this the face that launched a thousand ships/ And burnt the topmost towers of Ilium?" That's Marlowe's *Doctor Faustus.*

Watkins: Can that be of any advantage to a reader who did not catch the allusions on his own?

Manley: I don't think it's necessary to know the allusions.

Watkins: I know. But it still may have an effect on me, though I do not know the allusion which led partly to the quality of the poetry.

Manley: Yes.

Watkins: You were working in the same exalted terms and using their exalted style to exalt your own.

Manley: That's right.

Watkins: I had in mind still another. You don't think of any more?

Manley: No, I don't think of any more.

Watkins: It seems to me that Heliogabalus's attitude and stature and arrogance resemble those of Shelley's "Ozymandias."

Manley: Well, that's true. The complete arrogance and pride of rule. It's mostly a similarity of theme. But I certainly wasn't thinking of "Ozymandias." I was thinking of imperial pride and arrogance and then the crushing of it.

Watkins: Why would such a monster as Heliogabalus believe in such a supernatural thing as an oracle?

Manley: I don't know, but everyone at the time would seek out oracles. I suppose it's the curiosity to know the future. It doesn't mean necessarily that he believes in a supreme deity in the same way you and I may believe in a supreme deity—an all-loving, all-compassing God. It may be he believes that there was just a kind of person or force or genius there that could tell him the future.

Watkins: Oh, the oracle was a person rather than some spirit speaking from a temple or a burning bush?

Manley: I don't know what it was. It could have been a person. The gods or the deity or whatever the force was would speak through a personality who would go into a trance. Often they would shout down a crack, and echoes would come back. In the classical age it was nearly always a temple of some sort to one of the gods or another—Apollo or . . .

Watkins: Did you invent the ways that he thought of dying, or did he himself think of them?

Manley: It's a mixture of both. The Nubian slave may have been—I can't remember whether that was Heliogabalus's or not. But certainly the jewels are mine. I think he did build the tower, but the description of the tower is mine.

Watkins: What is a carbuncle?

Manley: A carbuncle is a kind of garnet, a very deep, pigeon-blood red garnet.

Watkins: "Easy ways to die/ Coiled in the cunning hollow of a ring"—those were poisons in the hollow of the ring? He would have to take them out and swallow them?

Manley: Yes. He would slip his ring in his mouth and then swallow them.

Watkins: The images of the tower of death are rich—"the swirling grain of the scaffolding"—did he have such a thing made, or did you invent it?

Manley: I made that up. He had a tower, but I made up the grain.

Watkins: What's "swirling grain"?

Manley: Heliogabalus gilded the wood, but he left the grain. He put gold leaf on it so that you could see the grain of the wood outlined in gold.

Watkins: Was it a tree also that had great difficulty growing, and the grain is twisted or "swirling"?

Manley: That's what I was thinking of. It was a very grainy wood, but he had put gold on it.

Watkins: Is your mind or history the source for the privy?

Manley: I believe that he really was put in a privy.

Watkins: And what was the "cunning hollow"? Is that to say that all privies are cunning hollows for deposits, or did he have one made with an enclosure where he could hide on the side?

Manley: I tried to suggest he was like an embryo inside a privy. He was hiding there, and it was a cunning hollow because he thought it would be very cunning to hide there. As I remember it, historically he did run into a privy to hide. He was found and killed. But I don't think he fell into the pit. I think that was my little touch.

Watkins: Why did you add that?

Manley: I just wanted to make it worse. I was also thinking of the cunning hollow of the privy like the cunning hollow of a ring. I wanted an echo there—a big difference between the way he really did die and the way he wanted to die.

Watkins: You were thinking of the difference between the materials of the emeralds, diamonds, and carbuncles and the materials in the pit?

Manley: Exactly. I think the sewer is historic. They did try to stuff him inside a sewer. The idea of transporting the body and trying to stuff it in places and get rid of it is what I was interested in.

Watkins: So as Heliogabalus was killed you were thinking of what life ironically gives him as compared to what he wants.

Manley: Right. He wanted fame, glory forever for the elegance of his death.

Watkins: The hiding in the hollow of a privy is a stark contrast with being dressed in imperial purple.

Manley: Well, he's willing to escape if he can. That's what he's trying to do in the privy.

Watkins: Are you saying in the poem that man reaches the condition as he thinks of dying where he doesn't care whether it is a carbuncle or a pit?

Manley: No. I was thinking that he didn't want to die. A person will do anything to stay, and that's what he's trying to do— escape the whole thing. No matter what preparation you make, there is no way to control the end. No matter what greatness and glory and esteem you achieve in this world, it's going to be stripped from you. What I'm talking about is the general situation—my own experiences with fame, glory, wealth, and my own personal realization that these things are not actual parts of a person.

Watkins: Did they really call him "Big Ass" and "Shit Face"?

Manley: No. I added that. "Big Ass," I guess, because he couldn't fit in the sewer, and "Shit Face" obviously. It is true that the soldiers who killed him couldn't speak any Latin. They were mercenaries who spoke barbaric tongues.

Watkins: Mercenaries or were they Goths?

Manley: They were some kind of mercenaries whether they came from the Gothic tribes or the straight Germans or whether they came from the Near East or Far East or whatever. They were mercenaries, and yet they were the central Roman legions—the Praetorian Guard. Rome was going downhill. Romans were not serving in the army. One of the things Heliogabalus wanted to do was to achieve fame in his dying, and here the people who killed him couldn't even speak the language, and the Senate ordered his name erased as though he had never existed.

Watkins: You take that through step after step: they couldn't speak his name, the senate ordered his name erased, they called him terrible names, he becomes a myth. But only while the story holds up. It moves steadily to forgetfulness and abstraction, and then the last line of the poem is . . .

Manley: "And then they forgot him."

Watkins: So you move from imperial purple to the pit to being forgotten.

Manley: Then the last part. There are some who still remember him, but they don't remember him for what he wanted to be remembered for. They remember him as he is presented in the poem, as an example of a man who couldn't control anything.

Watkins: Where did you get the "freckled hand"?

Manley: That comes from *Macbeth*. (Laughs.)

Watkins: Where is it in *Macbeth*?

Manley: At the end. This has always puzzled me—I never knew what it meant—but it's an interesting image. At the end of *Macbeth*, his head is chopped off, the head of a tyrant. And they bring it out, and they hold it by the hair at the end of the play. And Macduff says, "The time is free," as they hold that head up.

Watkins: And you don't know what that means?

Manley: Not really. It's as though time had gone into some kind of paroxysm in the play and now had freed itself. That seems to be what it suggests. It relates to the whole problem of the natural and unnatural that runs in the play that I don't fully understand.

Watkins: Could it be that no matter what era, history, or ruler will come into power in the next days, the time is at least free of this tyrant?

Manley: Free of Heliogabalus. I also meant it to suggest that time is free in the sense that it's part of that whole other order no one has any control over whatsoever.

Watkins: How is that free?

Manley: Because you can't change it.

Watkins: Oh, time is free of *us*.

Manley: Of us. Of our control. It's beyond us, you know. I think any thoughtful person would have to realize that what he does is surrounded by a very strange, mysterious otherness— some other force or other dimension. I thought of time as signifying that.

Watkins: Obviously, you were greatly impressed by Shakespeare's effective image of the freckled hand. You liked that so that you not only kept the hand dangling the head, but you kept the freckles on it.

Manley: I think I made them up.

Watkins: Shakespeare didn't have the freckles on the hand?

Manley: I don't think he did. No. I was thinking of a Scotchman having freckles. (Laughs.)

Watkins: You can put freckles on a Roman who doesn't have them?

Manley: I could if I wanted, but I'm not really specifying a Scotchman here. I'm just giving a kind of detail. If you look at his hand, you might see some freckles on it.

Watkins: The freckles matter to me a great deal.

Manley: Do they?

Watkins: First, one should always look for the literal: I see that hand better because it has freckles on it.

Manley: That's all I wanted.

Watkins: I don't believe it. As one sees the freckles, he sees more than freckles. Didn't you see more than freckles?

Manley: Yes, I mean it to be a kind of dream image—a universal symbol that we're going to get our heads chopped off.

Watkins: Cleopatra's hand didn't have freckles, did it?

Manley: No. I was thinking of some masculine hand.

Watkins: But it picks up more than masculinity. It picks up imperfections as well.
Manley: All right. It does. You're right.
Watkins: Imperfections on beauty.
Manley: Yes.
Watkins: You weren't thinking of that when you wrote the poem?
Manley: No.
Watkins: Is it in the poem?
Manley: I don't know, Floyd.
Watkins: Well, you just agreed with me that imperfections would not be on Cleopatra. Yet when they are on a hand carrying a head, you admitted that the hand is imperfect. Is that just a lucky accident?
Manley: I don't know. I just wanted to end the poem with a universal image that would apply what happened to Heliogabalus to everybody.
Watkins: Well, I'd rather have a smooth right hand than this big brown spot on mine and these beginning age marks. I think that some of those freckles may bear some of the qualities of what Heliogabalus fell into when he fell into the pit.
Manley: It could be. As I say, the only thing I thought of was making it specific. I was also thinking of Macduff's hand, a Scotchman having freckles. I didn't carry it any further, but I can see how you might very well.
Watkins: The ingredient is there in life, and the mind of the poet does not have to make every interpretation for himself.
Manley: I did think of the head like a lantern. This was a kind of illumination, a light to see the poem by. I see this as a very ironic poem because the only way Heliogabalus is remembered is in this way—despite all his glory, all his wealth, all his fame. A poem I wrote recently about Zenobia is related to this poem. I didn't realize it until just this minute. But Zenobia was captured. She was a queen captured by the Romans and made to walk in a triumph. She had to wear all her riches on her body, and then they stripped her. She had to wear all her ropes of jewels and pearls and furs.
Watkins: Do you like some of your poems more than others? Is this one of your favorites?
Manley: I think it may be a little extreme. Some parts of it—

like putting Heliogabalus in the privy and having the people call him "Big-Ass" and "Shit-Face"—go a little too far. I may have pushed it a little too hard.

Watkins: Are you saying that poetry sometimes cannot go as far as life?

Manley: Maybe. I pushed him into the privy. It may have been too much to add those touches.

Watkins: I know from people who saw it that the American soldiers on Attu sexually mutilated the corpses of Japanese soldiers. And I have heard that of other battles.

Manley: I have heard that.

Watkins: If you were writing a poem about the battle of Attu, would that image be too extreme?

Manley: Just because it happened doesn't mean that it couldn't be too extreme for a poem.

Watkins: Is there any criterion in poetry for extremism of imagery?

Manley: I think it has something to do with the poem itself. This is a rich and opulent poem.

Watkins: I heard a critic say about a certain poem and a certain poet that he was not sure the poet had earned his meaning. Is that what you mean?

Manley: Something like that.

Watkins: Still, that is an extremely subjective statement: one critic may believe one thing and another another.

Manley: That's true. In the first part of the poem I built very rich opulent imagery for a purpose, and I think that works well. Then I think I was tempted to build the opposite imagery, just as much in the opposite direction, and that wasn't necessary.

Watkins: I think it was. The poem earned the pit and the "Big Ass" and the "Shit Face."

Manley: All right. Then the poem in that respect works better for you than it does for me. I admit that when I finished it I liked it.

Erasmus in Love

Cras amet qui nunquam amavit quique amavit
Cras amet, Erasmus wrote. And then he reflected.
That girl across the room beside the stove,
That girl, he wrote, is in my head.
Those breasts I see are bulging in the sockets of my eyes.
This table too is in my head.
He reflected the table like the girl reflected the heat
Of the stove. These walls, these other people—
All in my head. She smiled, he wrote, smiling.
And now she's talking. Now she turns. Her rump
Slides on the chair, flattened out on each side,
Bulging. She leans forward. Her breasts dazzle
My eyes. The light falls from the air.

It's cold over here away from the stove, Erasmus
Wrote. The stove stinks like bacon grease.
Red with rust like raw skin. The people
Stink like the stove. The ice in the river freezes
In my veins. Who is that she's talking to?
Erasmus wrote. Why does she smile at him?
If this is all in my head, she ought
To smile at me, he reflected. Everyone
Else in the room—the farmers, the merchants, the
    travelers—
All leave to go to the bathroom at once.
Winter blasts in. We are suddenly alone.
She rocks her chair forward at me, leg
Tipping leg, and I reflect her coming,

He wrote, unbottoning her blouse. Her breasts
Swing free. She touches the nipple, smiling
At me. I am reflecting like a stove.
Winter blasts the room again. The people
Rush in. And she's back in her place at the stove.

Why does that always happen to me? Erasmus
Wrote. Why does everyone always come back
From the bathroom? Why do I always reflect things
Like that? he reflected. I should have said,
Here, let me help you, or, Hello, I am Erasmus.
Who are you, inching your chair over at me,
Touching your nipples, spreading your legs? But how
Was I to know it wasn't in my head
When everything else I see is there—this table,
These people, who never go to the bathroom anymore?
And whose head am I in? Erasmus wrote,
And why do you always do this to me?
Why do you send her here, and others like her,
Wherever I go? They ride up on mules, sleek
And naked as the flanks of beasts. Eyes like cows.
Udders like goats. They make obscene gestures in upstairs
Windows, come out of dark woods, behind
Trees, around corners. They come at me
In my sleep and always walk past me, Erasmus
Wrote, because I suspect they are in my head.

All of a sudden he put down the pen and stared
Across the room at me. I tried to look busy,
The checkers suddenly complicated as chess. I started
To talk to the girl again, asked her her name.
She shifted her hips and squirmed a little. Erasmus
Still stared. So I figured, what the hell.
I took her by the hand and led her over.
I leaned forward. His breath smelled like fish.

I said, are you the illustrious Desiderius Erasmus
Of Rotterdam, Light of the North? Yes, indeed, he said,
I am. Fingers twitching. I said, let me
Introduce to you Marilyn de Kooning. Delighted,
He murmured. I have often admired you from afar.

The breasts you point I have cupped in my hands.
The hands you hold in your lap like pigeons,
I have seen above my head making signs
From top-story windows. Your eyes have ridden
Before me over the Alps. I dreamed of you once
In More's garden, and at banquets of kings and great
Princes, you were under the table at work.
Excuse me a moment, Erasmus said, and he picked
Up the pen. His eyes turned inward.
He started to fade, like light after sunset.
She stands up, Erasmus wrote, swings
A shawl around her head. Skin translucent
As the stove. She walks across the room.
Her ass shimmers like heat, and I am reflecting.

Years later, in the portrait by Dürer, his skin
Pouchy as unbaked bread, arthritic fingers
Like tendrils twisted beside a bowl of flowers,
Erasmus wrote a gloss on a love poem,
Explaining that it is all in your head.
Love will come in a rushing of wind, he wrote.
Lust will leap in your veins like a goat over
A fence, and you will see her, Erasmus wrote,
Naked as the sky in the summer. She will shimmer like
heat
Coming toward you and say, Erasmus, Erasmus mine,
I waited for you beside the great oaks
On the roadway I heard you would pass.
I lingered at wells while my parents called in the dark.

I saw you from my bedroom window, with my husband
Asleep on the bed beside me. I waved at you
And showed you my name, gave you a sign of my love.
I have dipped my handkerchief in my own blood
And wiped your saddle, cut my hair and bound it
To the tail of your horse to draw you to me.
I sat across from you in the stove rooms
Of innumerable inns while you wrote and looked
But did not see. And now you are mine
Erasmus wrote. We will love here forever.

This was in Washington, in the National Gallery.
I saw the wild flowers, the aged desperate
Face and took out a piece of paper
And began to write. He took off his clothes, I wrote,
His cassock, his ermine, even the hard-earned stones
On his fingers. He laid them neatly in a pile
And walked toward her, shaking the wrinkles loose
As he went, shedding his skin like smoke in the winter.
She shimmered before him like sunset on fast-moving
    water.
When the guard got to me, I had her dress
Halfway up her hip. A scream panicked
Inside her throat like the sounds of hoofs in a pen,
And I thought, Erasmus, you old bastard you.

The Man Within

Watkins: In your poems about historical figures, how much do you add to the facts?

Manley: A good bit. I take a germ of historical fact and build on that. I change history, make it do what I want it to. I do not feel responsible to historical fact.

Watkins: Poets are not responsible, or you are not responsible?

Manley: I am not responsible. I can't speak for other people.

Watkins: You take an event or a situation and then work imaginatively with character and motivation. Is that right?

Manley: Sometimes I do that, and sometimes I do other things.

Watkins: Such as?

Manley: Sometimes a situation reminds me of something in another context, and I bring that other context in, and it changes it.

Watkins: Was the poem about Erasmus mostly invention?

Manley: Yes.

Watkins: In what sense?

Manley: Well, it's all invention. (Laughs.)

Watkins: Then why in the world did you name it for Erasmus?

Manley: I wrote a number of poems on Erasmus. For a while, I was writing Erasmus poems.

Watkins: What brought that about?

Manley: I don't know. I just started writing poems about Erasmus.

Watkins: You had been reading him?

Manley: No. I was reading a lot of Thomas More. I've not read that much Erasmus, but he was a friend of More's, and I always thought of them as different from each other. Erasmus always seemed to me the archetypical scholar.

Watkins: You don't like archetypical scholars?

Manley: I don't have absolute respect for them.

Watkins: What's their problem?

Manley: They're too analytical, too rational, too *prideful*. Erasmus was a very successful man in his day. He got everything he ever wanted. Great adulation, great fame while he lived, but not the same kind of fame Thomas More achieved.

Watkins: Was Erasmus too much a man of the head?

Manley: Yes. That's it exactly.

Watkins: And too little a man of what?

Manley: Of the body, the senses.

Watkins: Do you think, like John Crowe Ransom or maybe T. S. Eliot, that one should be a full and whole man? Is this poem partly about that?

Manley: Yes.

Watkins: Could you tell me something about Erasmus or could you find a quotation that could demonstrate briefly something of his rationalism and incompleteness?

Manley: No one quotation would do it. The problem was the kind of work he did—all textual work—all scholarly.

Watkins: What kind of textual work did he do?

Manley: He translated and edited the New Testament and wrote a commentary on it.

Watkins: Pedantically?

Manley: No. For its time, it was very *un*pedantic. But like all scholarship, there was a lot of pedantry involved.

Watkins: Will you translate the Latin at the beginning?

Manley: Yes. It is from the *Pervigilium Veneris,* a poem of late classical antiquity. It means the Eve of Venus or, as some people translate it, St. Venus's Eve. It's a poem written for a fertility festival about the anticipation of love-making. It says: "Tomorrow those will love who never have loved, and those who have loved before will love again tomorrow."

Watkins: You say Erasmus wrote the love poem though somebody else actually did it?

Manley: That's right.

Watkins: I see. What kind of man did you make him in your poem?

Manley: I described him as very taken with women, but very unsuccessful. He doesn't make it.

Watkins: Or them.

Manley: That's right. He's obsessed by them.

Watkins: And you have no evidence at all in history, biography, his life, that he was obsessed by them?

Manley: *Au contraire!* I don't know about Erasmus's sex life, but I don't think there was much of it.

Watkins: Do you give him any sex life in the poem?

Manley: Well, a lot of imagined sex life.

Watkins: I see. You are playing with the man, having fun teasing a historical figure although you think it very possible that there wasn't even very much imagined sex life in his life.

Manley: That's right.

Watkins: Then this is a joke on Erasmus.

Manley: I guess so. As a friend of mine who is a great Erasmus scholar said, "This is not the Erasmus I know."

Watkins: Well, it's not really the one you know historically either, but the one you made up—your invention.

Manley: Yes, that's right.

Watkins: Was Erasmus a Catholic priest?

Manley: Yes. He was a monk and the illegitimate son of a priest.

Watkins: He was therefore supposed to be celibate.

Manley: Yes.

Watkins: And you have no evidence of any lack of celibacy in his entire life.

Manley: No.

Watkins: What was the beginning of the conception of this poem, Frank? Why did you think, "I'll do this to old Erasmus"? How in the world did you think of the joke?

Manley: Well, I was really contrasting him with More in my mind. Erasmus once wrote to More and said that he was not a martyr, nothing like a martyr, and never would be or could be and had no interest in it. He was just not willing to commit himself that deeply or that much to anything.

Watkins: If he had had a life dedicated to his beliefs, you wouldn't have thought of a joke on him?

Manley: No. The lack of passion in Erasmus—I mean—intellectual or physical or any kind of passionate commitment—that's really what I was writing about.

Watkins: So the poem has that serious purpose beyond being merely a joke on Erasmus?

Manley: Yes. It's also a poem, I guess, about me because I'm a scholar, too, you know. And it's about my distrusting my own rational apparatus.

Watkins: Oh, you are yourself too rational and celibate?

Manley: Yes. (Big laugh from both.) All of us in this business share a little of Erasmus in us. The persona was interesting to me for that reason: it spoke to some parts of my personality that I'm suspicious of. What I don't like about people in academic life is the excessive rationality and analytical cast of mind. We're trained to be coldly analytical. So I respond negatively to Erasmus.

Watkins: When Erasmus says "Those breasts I see are bulging in the sockets of my eyes" and "her breasts dazzle/ My eyes"—when you say those things, that is another kind of disapproval. Erasmus never is a balanced man.

Manley: That's right. Yes. But it's not just a poem about sex. It's a poem about the lack of sex in Erasmus's life. He never has fullness. It's only fantasy, only mentalized still, with him.

Watkins: Well, what else should he have done besides chase women to be a complete man, Frank?

Manley: He shouldn't have had so much of it happening just in his mind.

Watkins: What else should he have happening?

Manley: I mean, he ought to have taken the irrational aspects of his personality into account, his physical life.

Watkins: He should have chopped wood sometimes?

Manley: Yes. He should have made more use of his body instead of just sitting there scribbling all the time.

Watkins: (Pauses.) Is this poem a dramatic monologue?

Manley: No. Erasmus talks parts of it, but there is another personality in the poem—me. The poem says, "All of a sudden he put down the pen and stared/ Across the room at me. I tried to look busy. . . ."

Watkins: Who is that?

Manley: That's me, the speaker of the poem. I tried to look busy. I'm sitting on the other side of the room playing checkers, and then I start to talk to the girl that he's been looking at. I ask her her name, and she shifts her hips and squirms a little, and Erasmus is still staring at her.

Watkins: Were you, too, attracted by her rump sliding on the chair?

Manley: Oh, well, sure! That's why I'm talking to her! (Laughter all round.) I am actually talking to the girl that Erasmus would like to talk to. Erasmus is across the room staring at her.

Watkins: Oh, I see. Does the poem ever tell what you're talking about?

Manley: No.

Watkins: Did you have in mind what you were talking about?

Manley: No. (Laughter.) But I did know that I was talking to the girl when Erasmus wasn't.

Watkins: And you did know what you *wanted* to talk to the girl about?

Manley: Yes. That's right. It's the difference between accomplishment and lack of accomplishment. So I feel sorry for Erasmus and introduce the girl to him.

Watkins: Yet the whole subject is on the full man, and the poem is no more licentious than it is celibate, in your judgment. It's not about sex, but it is about fullness.

Manley: That's right.

Watkins: By the way, what was the country of the poem?

Manley: The scene of it is what was known in the Renaissance as the *hypocaust*, that is, the stove room. Humanists like Erasmus referred to it as the *hypocaust*. Public inns had one room they kept the stove in, and everyone crowded into that room and stayed there in the wintertime, in Germany.

Watkins: I would have thought Erasmus would have stayed away from such places.

Manley: It was a place to get warm, a place to be around people, and of course it would really smell *strong*. But humanists went there in winter and wrote. I translated a book by Richard Pace, and he said he wrote it in a *hypocaust* in Switzerland.

Watkins: When you wrote about Erasmus and his speaking and then put in the character "I," were you aware of what you were doing poetically and technically? Does it just come to you intuitively, or do you think that you will write a poem in a particular kind of genre?

Manley: No, it just happened. I don't even understand the poem, quite frankly. I mean, I don't understand a lot of the convolutions in it.

Watkins: Give me an example.

Manley: Well, Erasmus is writing inside the poem. He's writing the poem, but the I is also in the room. The I who is writing the poem is also in the room with Erasmus talking to him. So I don't know who is writing the poem. Then at the end of the poem, the police take me away.

Watkins: What do they take you away for?

Manley: Because I slip my hand up a woman's dress.

Watkins: I see.

Manley: Because I've been looking at a portrait of Erasmus on the wall. So there are a lot of convolutions that I don't really understand.

Watkins: But they are technical convolutions rather than philosophical and theological convolutions?

Manley: No. Something like philosophical convolutions.

Watkins: I have a convolution I want you to explain: " 'If this is all in my head, she ought/ To smile at me,' he reflected."

Manley: Yes. Erasmus knows that reality is what he thinks it is, especially when he writes it. And therefore if he's making up everything and makes up this woman, then she ought to be smiling at him, because he ought to have at least enough sense to make her do that if he's making it all happen. But it was never successful, the women remain imaginary, and I feel sorry for him. I think he missed a lot.

Watkins: You *pity* him.

Manley: Yes, that's right.

Watkins: But you feel no love for him.

Manley: That's right.

Watkins: Does he imagine the people come from the bathroom?

Manley: Yes.

Watkins: "All leave to go to the bathroom at once." How's that possible?

Manley: It isn't. He makes it up. He wants to vacate the room so that he can have the woman. He sends everybody out to go to the bathroom at once, but then they all come back, and he doesn't understand that.

Watkins: You're not working with any Berkeleyan ideas in your statement about Erasmus's belief that things are "in the head"?

Manley: Yes. That's what I'm thinking about. I'm thinking of Berkley: whatever your reality is is what you project. It has to do with fantasy, I guess.

Watkins: In the question, "Why do you always do this to me?" who are you?

Manley: It's like he's asking me who is writing the poem. He can't understand why he can't make connections with these women.

Watkins: Is there an actual unbuttoning of the blouse, or is that in his mind?

Manley: It's hard, I think, to tell what's happening and what isn't happening in the poem. I imagined this to be happening in his mind.

Watkins: Who does the unbuttoning?

Manley: She does it after he writes that she does it (laughs)—if that makes any sense. He creates her to do it, and then she does it. What I wanted to do was have the reader not know, Floyd, and the kind of question you're asking is the kind of question I don't want the poem to answer. I want people to wonder.

Watkins: Am I reading it wrongly or rightly by wondering?

Manley: You're absolutely right in wondering, but I think you can't get an answer.

Watkins: Okay. I'll buy that. After your break, "All of a sudden he put down the pen and stared/ Across the room at me." Who put down the pen?

Manley: Erasmus.

Watkins: Who's speaking?

Manley: I am, the poet.

Watkins: But it's not the poet; it's the persona; you're not back in Erasmus's time.

Manley: No, except for the fact that I imagined Erasmus to be in that time, and therefore I'm there, too.

Watkins: So you put yourself imaginatively in that room and you see Erasmus stare across the room at you.

Manley: Erasmus saw the woman, because he was writing about the woman; so I see Erasmus because I am writing about Erasmus. And if I see Erasmus, Erasmus sees me.

Watkins: There are a lot of remarkable steps of the imagination here.

Manley: What I'm playing around with is the idea that what you create has its effect on you.

Watkins: Is this fish Friday?

Manley: You mean the fact that he smells like fish?

Watkins: That's what I'm deriving it from.

Manley: No. I wasn't thinking of that.

Watkins: He hasn't been eating fish; he just stinks.

Manley: He just smells like fish. That's right.

Watkins: I see. Where did you get the name Marilyn de Kooning?

Manley: Erasmus is Dutch, and I wanted a Dutch name, and then I thought of the great Dutch contemporary painter, De Kooning, Wilhelm de Kooning, who did some very interesting portraits of women that became kind of explosive. I was interested in those portraits for a long time. De Kooning would begin with a portrait of Marilyn Monroe, and it would become a monstrous grotesque. So I was making a very buried allusion to Marilyn Monroe and Wilhelm de Kooning.

Watkins: What do you mean by "the breasts you point"?

Manley: Just that some breasts are pointy breasts.

Watkins: Who has "cupped them in his hands"?

Manley: Erasmus.

Watkins: How about the poet?

Manley: No, the poet's not there. This is just Erasmus.

Watkins: Are you being prudish, now?

Manley: No, no. This is in the poem; that's Erasmus. He can't really make contact with a real woman, because of the tremendous imagined life he's leading.

Watkins: He has cupped the breasts in his hands in his mind.

Manley: In his mind, right.

Watkins: What is the place of sex in this poem?

Manley: I don't think it is a very erotic poem. In this poem, I think of sex as mostly having to do with animal vitality.

Watkins: So sex in poetry may be extraordinarily lustful and sexy, but it also has in all your poems a symbolic meaning—various moral and aesthetic meanings?

Manley: Yes.

Watkins: Explain "I am reflecting."

Manley: It's a kind of pun.

Watkins: "Her ass shimmers like heat, and I am reflecting. . . ."

Manley: I mean that he's thinking: "I am reflecting on her ass shimmering like heat." I didn't think of Erasmus as being so much aroused as he was fascinated. I think of Erasmus in this poem as being frustrated instead of aroused. Fascinated, interested, and frustrated all simultaneously. Her ass shimmers like heat, and he's reflecting that heat back.

Watkins: He doesn't have any heat, but he can maybe reflect a little.

Manley: He's reflecting her physicality. The same way the stove does the same thing. "I am reflecting like a stove," he says earlier.

Watkins: Is there a portrait by Dürer?

Manley: Yes.

Watkins: What does seeing the painting add to the reading of the poem?

Manley: It's an engraving or etching. It's not a painting. It says in a Latin inscription on it that it was done from life. That is, Erasmus sat for it. It was a life study. He's holding an inkpot, and he's writing, and he has books on the table and some wild flowers, but he's very old, and I wanted an image of Erasmus as an aged man.

Watkins: Wouldn't it be a better poem if you had a younger man?

Manley: I don't think so. I wanted to indicate that this frustration had gone on all his life.

Watkins: It does not come from his impotent old age?

Manley: No, no. It's been going on, and this is years later after this event in the stove room. Years later he's still the same thing. What I imagined Erasmus to be writing in that portrait is a gloss on a love poem, and what he's saying is that love is all in your head. But what I've been trying to indicate is that it *isn't* all in your head because "her ass shimmers like heat," and he just reflects it. There's something out there really happening, but he's incapable of grabbing it up, incapable of doing it, because he's so much in his head.

Watkins: To what degree is this a comic poem, a serious poem, and a mixture?

Manley: I guess it's a mixture. I think of Erasmus as being a kind of comic figure in a pitiful way. And that's where the poem gets serious.

Watkins: But not tragic?

Manley: No, not tragic.

Watkins: Not high enough to be tragic.

Manley: That's right. He just wasted opportunities.

Watkins: Why do you introduce the husband so late? I had been thinking that one need not have worried about a husband with this woman, and then you have her married. "I saw you from my bedroom. . . ."

Manley: Oh, that's just one of them. One of them was married. But there are others. Look at this one: "I lingered at wells, while my parents called in the dark." It's many different women who are all one woman. One of them was a young girl; one of them was an older woman.

Watkins: Now the last three lines: "I have dipped my handkerchief in my own blood/ And wiped your saddle, cut my hair and bound it/ To the tail of your horse to draw you to me." Is that Manley or folklore, invention or medieval thinking or what?

Manley: That's Manley imagining medieval folklore.

Watkins: Is it menstrual blood?

Manley: Yes. That's what I thought.

Watkins: You thought at the time it was menstrual blood.

Manley: Menstrual blood, right. They wanted to attract him, and these were devices whereby they thought they would do it. But they never did, and that is why I take pity on him in his old age and finish the poem by having him run toward the woman shedding his wrinkles and clothes as he goes. And then what I'm doing catches up with me. Along with the other things we've mentioned, this is also a poem about how the things we do turn on us. We think we're doing them, but all of a sudden they turn around, and we find out that they are doing us. And that's what happens at the end—to me and Erasmus.

In the Mountains

Ghost Story

They asked for it, safe in their flannel cocoons
For the night, prepared to sleep and dream
Into their chrysalis of day.

So I told them of Tickanately Church,
That sits high on the flashing river,
Washed with the blood of its burying ground,
And how its lonely bell would ring
That very night, when long nails
Scratched at the pine of the coffin
Till clod by clod the grave unburied itself
And the shapeless thing took shape again,
Rising to scatter the plastic flowers
And all the names turned into stone at
    Tickanately Church,
Slashing the ground with its long nails
In the immortal, mysterious hate of the dead.

And suddenly I scared myself.
I saw myself in the lonely clay of Tickanately
    Church,
Tearing the flowers my children brought
On sunlit days in the upper air,
While close in the night,
In the house made tight with the strength of my
    arms,
My children slept into age.

Decoration Day

Watkins: What is a ghost?

Manley: A person, a spirit, who comes back from the dead and haunts this earth.

Watkins: Do you believe that?

Manley: No, though I'm interested in it as a representation of an idea I have.

Watkins: Do some people believe in ghosts?

Manley: Yes.

Watkins: What kind of people?

Manley: Children and people who are susceptible to believing in extraterrestrial phenomena, ESP, flying saucers, witches. Some people believe more than others. I suspect ignorance has nothing to do with it.

Watkins: Is a ghost story a literary form?

Manley: Sure.

Watkins: If you were defining the genre, what would you say about it?

Manley: It is a narrative, usually told to children. Adults don't sit around having drinks and telling ghost stories unless it occurs as an oddity in conversation. Maybe in more primitive societies they were more prevalent.

Watkins: Do ghost stories attain converts during the telling, converts to a kind of belief in some kind of supernatural?

Manley: Perhaps for the moment of telling.

Watkins: Did you hear ghost stories as a child in Atlanta?

Manley: Yes.

Watkins: Are they for sophisticated adults too?

Manley: No. They're for people who have a kind of oral tradition, people who don't read much and who still carry on more primitive folkways.

Watkins: Are they traditional or invented at the moment?

Manley: Most are traditional. Some may be improvised from a certain scrap of fact.

Watkins: Here you improvised a ghost story and then composed a poem about it?

Manley: Right.

Watkins: Do you think ghosts are more at home in the country in Gilmer County, Georgia, than in Atlanta?

Manley: Yes. An interesting book done by a local historian in Gilmer County is called *Ghost Stories from the Southern Mountains.* It'a little paperback the man had printed himself. He tells ghost stories that aren't very scary or very good, but they're ghosts he knows about.

Watkins: The more scary, credible, and believable, the better?

Manley: Right.

Watkins: Did your children ask for a ghost story as you say in the poem? Did they want to be scared?

Manley: They wanted a spooky story. Children like to be scared sometimes.

Watkins: Do they want the thrill in retrospect or do they want the experience of the moment of having it?

Manley: Just the scariness of it at the time.

Watkins: What is their "chrysalis of day"?

Manley: It means that they're still in the process of becoming what they are going to be, and they've moved from one cocoon into another cocoon—the flannel snuggies.

Watkins: That's an exact description of a warm child being put to bed. Do you think "chrysalis of day" occurs during their whole childhood—day and night?

Manley: What I wanted to indicate was that they continued to be in a kind of protective atmosphere, not only at night when they were snug in bed but also in the daytime as children.

Watkins: Not as adults?

Manley: As adults they would change into something else.

Watkins: Is there a real Tickanately Church?

Manley: Yes.

Watkins: Where is it?

Manley: About four miles from my home, off Roy Road in Gilmer County, on the way to Doublehead Gap. Those roads are paved now. The road to Doublehead Gap is paved, and the county commissioner in the last election paved every side road as far as the church. (Laughs.)

Watkins: Do you think he may have destroyed some ghosts by paving?

Manley: You're talking about the loss of the primitive ways of the place? They're going out of existence.

Watkins: I knew of a tree where a man had hanged himself. When that tree fell or when it was cut down probably the ghost and the ghost story disappeared.

Manley: I'm sure that happened.

Watkins: Ghosts have their homes and haunts. What is the source of the name Tickanately?

Manley: I guess Indian, named for a creek.

Watkins: Are there other Indian names of that sort in the area, such as the Cartecay River? Do you know what that name means?

Manley: No.

Watkins: Do you know any other Indian names that seem so mysterious?

Manley: I believe Noontootley is. Ellijay. I've heard two or three meanings of Ellijay. And then there's the Coosawattee River.

Watkins: Do you think they pick up their beauty as names because of their foreignness to us or because they had a beauty to the Indian too? When they're translated, I find beauty in the translation.

Manley: I don't think of Tickanately as a beautiful name. I wanted to give the idea of a church that would be typical of the place. In fact, I'm not really describing the churchyard at Tickanately Church. I'm describing the churchyard at Scroogetown Church, a different church entirely.

Watkins: Scroogetown. An English name?

Manley: I don't know. I've seen it on maps written Seteuge, which sounds Indian to me.

Watkins: I wonder if it's my association with Ebenezer Scrooge that makes it sound stingy to me.

Manley: I named the church Tickanately because I wanted some other name than Scroogetown.

Watkins: Have you ever heard old-timers refer to the strange names in that section of the country?

Manley: Some of them they translate. There's a mountain near us named for an Indian town called Turniptown. That was translated into English.

Watkins: The Indians had turnips there?

Manley: That must have been why it was called Turniptown.

Watkins: The turnip is not an Indian, an American plant, is it?

Manley: I don't know. I just assumed the Indians raised turnips there. But maybe not.

Watkins: What does "washed with the blood of its burying ground" mean?

Manley: I wanted to get the idea of some other river flowing. There's one river flowing near the church. That's the Cartecay River. And the church itself has its river of the generations of people who are buried there.

Watkins: Did you have in mind any connection with the Christian idea of being "washed in the blood of the lamb"?

Manley: It may have worked that way unconsciously. One river led into another. The river of blood. Of course there's the old hymn about the fountain of blood, the idea of baptism as being washed in the blood of the Lamb. I don't know how conscious I was of that.

Watkins: Did this church have a church bell?

Manley: Yes. It had a kind of steeple. The Scroogetown Church was an old school at one time, and it has a bizarre kind of steeple. It looks as if it has been tacked on to it, added later. I don't know whether it has a bell, but a bell tower sits on top of the schoolhouse.

Watkins: Are you telling the children how the bell will ring with a lonely sound that very night?

Manley: Yes. I was telling about Tickanately Church and about the bell and what was going to happen that night.

Watkins: When did you plan this ghost story for the children? Had you planned it at the very moment of the telling?

Manley: No, we had been to the graveyard that day. We had walked around, and I found an arrowhead on one of the graves. It was a striking kind of place, and the kids said, "Tell a story, tell a story." So I started inventing one about the place we had just been. I made up a tale about what had come to hand that day.

Watkins: Why did the ghost come out of the grave? "The grave unburied itself / And the shapeless thing took shape again." Is that coming out the grave?

Manley: Right.

Watkins: Is that Resurrection morning or is that some non-religious, inexplicable ghostly thing?

Manley: That's a ghostly thing. I wanted to suggest that this was an annual occurrence: once a year this thing would come out of the grave. This was the very night of the event. A grave would undig itself, and this thing would come out and then tear up the graveyard.

Watkins: (Laughs. Both laugh.) You mean you had fun with this story as well as the ultimate fright which you described in the last sentence?

Manley: Yes. It was making up a bizarre story. They said make up a story; so that's all I could think of. I wanted to just have some ghostly occurrence.

Watkins: Well, what you *really* want is the ghost coming out the grave in the minds of the children.

Manley: Yes.

Watkins: And it so happened that you became so wrapped up in your story that it came out of the grave in your mind too?

Manley: That's right.

Watkins: You knew it wasn't true, but you half believed it. How would you describe that?

Manley: Sometimes you start telling or thinking up something, and it just strikes you very hard and you get scared.

Watkins: Even if you know it's not true.

Manley: Yes. But what it stands for is true.

Watkins: The thing "rises to scatter the plastic flowers." Do you and the ghost react the same way to the artificial flowers?

Manley: I think they're very strange. They're not part of my culture and my cultural expectations, but they are everywhere in north Georgia.

Watkins: Do you think they are part of the north Georgia culture?

Manley: I do.

Watkins: I don't. They are extraordinarily incongruent with the place. Does that make me different from the country people? I used to be one of them.

Manley: I don't know. I think they love them.

Watkins: My father didn't like them.

Manley: The graveyard at New Liberty Baptist Church had

just been decorated, and J. B. Eliot told me, "Go there and look at how beautiful it is." I went to see, and it was the most garish looking thing I have ever seen—plastic flowers everywhere.

Watkins: Don't you think there's something wrong with them besides the garishness?

Manley: It bothers me. It may not be an old folkway, but it's a current folkway.

Watkins: True. The flowers are an artificial and unnatural creation of man instead of nature or God. Is that behind it?

Manley: Yes. It has to do with taste too. People up in the mountains make quilts out of polyester doubleknit, you know. That bothers me a lot. It seems to be a phony kind of fabric, and it doesn't look good on a quilt. But they like the bright colors.

Watkins: Why did you put plastic flowers in the graveyard in the poem—besides the fact that the people put them there? Is it to have an effect on the children and you too?

Manley: We had just seen all these flowers, and they're a major part of the graveyard.

Watkins: Do they have anything to do with the ghost? Would the ghost hate the flowers?

Manley: The ghost hates everything. This ghost does. He comes out of the grave and he wants to destroy it all. He's just mad.

Watkins: Are you sexist; what made you make him a male?

Manley: Did I make him a male?

Watkins: You said *he.*

Manley: When I was talking about it, but I called it "it" in the poem. Perhaps I said *he* because I may identify with the ghost. (Both laugh).

Watkins: Why would you identify with the ghost—in order to scare the children more?

Manley: It's what happens in the poem. I identified with the ghost. I become the ghost.

Watkins: You are incarnated in the ghost?

Manley: Yes. I was thinking that the ghost was alien to people when it died. It gets up and destroys all the memories, all the memorials to itself, really.

Watkins: "Took shape again." Does that mean that it assumed some kind of physical or spiritual body?

Manley: I suppose a physical body.

Watkins: "Rising to scatter the plastic flowers"—because it hates everything, not because they are plastic flowers?

Manley: Not because they are plastic. He hates them because they are just there.

Watkins: What is the function of "all the names"? To scatter the flowers *and* the names? Does he scatter the gravestones as well as the flowers?

Manley: Right. I am describing a kind of anti-Decoration Day here. The ghost undoes everything that's done on Decoration Day.

Watkins: What is Decoration Day?

Manley: Decoration Day in the country has nothing to do with the graves of veterans of wars. It is the time once a year when all the people have a homecoming at the church and an all-day singing and dinner. They bring covered-dish dinners, and they decorate the graves. They put the plastic flowers on them and clean up the graveyard, tidy the graves, make it nice.

Watkins: Bring a hoe, cut down all the weeds, remake the mounds, and so forth. Now that's done in the city graveyard by a workman paid with money that comes from the system they call perpetual care. Have you ever known of a Decoration Day in Atlanta?

Manley: No.

Watkins: Of course, you have never participated in a Decoration Day because you're Catholic and never had any relatives buried in a country churchyard.

Manley: No. I never have. I've gone to Decoration Day, though.

Watkins: Do you have a personal reaction to this custom?

Manley: I think it's strange. They have preaching in the graveyard first and then the singing.

Watkins: *In* the graveyard rather than the church?

Manley: Yes, at New Liberty anyway. That's the only church I've gone to on Decoration Day.

Watkins: Is it a time of joy, like an Irish wake, or is it a time of new grief or both or a time of association between the people who come back?

Manley: The main thing is the association of the people who come back. Hubert Matthews and all his six boys come and participate in the activities of the church that day.

Watkins: There is expression of love for the dead by returning to the place of the dead.

Manley: Right. But I didn't see anyone weeping or any grief. One woman I was with, an old lady, J. B. Eliot's mother, has her tombstone already there, with her birthdate on it, but not her death date. She saw her own tombstone and was right there helping decorate it. Her husband is buried by the place where she will lie after she dies. People go around, take one flower, a plastic flower, and stick it into a grave if they are not making a big floral offering.

Watkins: Do any bring living flowers?

Manley: Never have. Sometimes you'll see a wilted bouquet of real flowers on a grave.

Watkins: This seems like a pleasant community scene. I don't understand one thing in your poem: the ghost's mysterious hate, the hate of the dead. What caused that?

Manley: I wanted to indicate alienness, differentness.

Watkins: He hates the flowers; he hates the tombstones. Does he hate the living for being alive?

Manley: Yes.

Watkins: Associating yourself with the ghost, you imagined yourself to be dead hating the living for being still alive?

Manley: Yes. That's what scared me.

Watkins: At the time of talking to your children you actually felt fear? You saw yourself in the lonely dead.

Manley: A little. Fear may not be the word, but I was taken by the image, the idea.

Watkins: When you think of yourself as dead, do you have a preference for one kind of cemetery over another?

Manley: I used to think that I wanted to be buried in one of those cemeteries up there in north Georgia. I am not certain of that any more. I may want to be cremated. I have always been disturbed by what happens in the grave. One of the things that bothers me most is walking away from a grave, leaving the person in it.

Watkins: Do you think that cremation may be more final?

Manley: It happens quicker than decomposition.

Watkins: Do you have any feeling of community in the associ-ation of the dead? Do the ghosts join the living who come back on Decoration Day? Is your cremation a giving up of the idea that those who know you would know where you were buried?

Manley: Yes.

Watkins: What happens in the last stanza? You scare yourself; you see yourself in the lonely clay. "Tearing the flowers my children brought"—now that's after you died and they brought flowers on Decoration Day for you. Why do you hate them?

Manley: That's a part of the mysterious hate the dead have. I am that thing in the grave, and I come out.

Watkins: Were your children frightened?

Manley: I don't think so. (Laughter.) It was not that good a ghost story unless you really thought about dying. I was the only one scared by it. Children don't think that much about dying.

Watkins: I disagree.

Manley: Well, maybe they do.

Watkins: Think of Vardaman in *As I Lay Dying* and Janet in John Crowe Ransom's "Janet Waking." Didn't you have a moment as a child of first feeling what death was and that it had to come to you?

Manley: I can remember when it happened with one of my children, but I can't remember with me.

Watkins: If your children sleep into age—the last line says "my children slept into age"—what happens to you?

Manley: I also die. I am also caught up in the same process of aging, and I will ultimately die, and they will ultimately wake up. That returns to the image of being in a cocoon or chrysalis. They are going to wake up as adults, and I'm going to die before they do.

Watkins: During the telling of the ghost story you became excruciatingly aware of the process of sleeping.

Manley: Yes. They are ultimately going to sleep after the story is told. That's what sleep means in one sense. In another sense, their childhood is a kind of sleep.

Watkins: So the ghost may be more horrible to the adult than the child. To the child it is simply a creation by Frankenstein, a pleasant monster. To you it becomes religious, supernatural, perhaps philosophical.

Manley: You can't put ghosts in a religious context very well.

Watkins: With the church and "washed with the blood of its burying ground," I can't escape religion in this, Frank. Or the lack of it. It may be a constant frame of reference in your life which crept into the poem and *is* there, but only because you have a religious cast of mind which you didn't consciously think of in the poem.

Manley: Could be. But you can't think of ghosts in a religious framework because souls in heaven are enjoying the sight of God, and souls in hell are being tortured by demons if you believe in hell. That doesn't leave any room for ghosts. They are nontheological, but in that graveyard they seem fitting. If I were to think theologically, I would think the dead should not hate the living. They ought to be enjoying the afterlife. I met an old man the other day who was eighty-seven years old. He was sitting on his porch, and I went up and talked to him. He had lived in that place all his life. He said, "I'm going soon to a better place." The old man was going to a better place. But this ghost wants to get back, you know. And hates it that he isn't alive.

Watkins: You and the ghost may not be able to think about going to a better place like the old man's.

Manley: Maybe.

Watkins: So the ghost story may represent a fear of a worse place?

Manley: (Laughs.) No, it isn't that. You talked about my having a religious cast of mind. I think I probably do, but it is also a very doubting religious cast of mind.

Watkins: Your doubt is also mingled with hope, isn't it?

Manley: I have both. Sometimes I can imaginatively perceive the dead as wanting to get alive again. In the *Odyssey*, there's an awful thing—a blood sacrifice where the ghosts of the heroic dead come wanting to lick up the blood. They want to have some sense of life again. They are thin and shadelike. These are the great heroes of the past who come wanting to do that. Sometimes I see that as a possibility. I have great doubts about the existence of God and the afterlife.

Watkins: Doubts that rise and fall and also moments of certainty?

Manley: That's right.

Watkins: Don't you think those come to the most devout believers?

Manley: I do.

Watkins: "Lord, I believe. Help thou my unbelief."

Manley: That's right. One of the significant things to me about this poem is the way in which there are different kinds of awakenings to different kinds of reality. One is the children being in a kind of sleep in their childhood, protected by a house or by parents or by their own childish innocence. Then they wake from that sleep into a kind of adulthood that is aware and knows like the person who tells the ghost story. And then another kind of awakening is in the ghost itself, the dead person. The ghost wakes to come back from the dead.

Watkins: And then your own awakening.

Manley: Yes. I awaken into all these different states of reality—all the difficult things the poem sets forth—and I hope the reader does too.

Ghost

For Ben Mathis

In every nail sunk into every board,
In every sill levered there,
The muscles of my back still hold it up.
And my hands shape the waters that still fall
From the molded pine of the trough at the spring.
My mind turned on the lights,
Like tendons ran the wires where the current flows,
Cut the glass and placed the windowpanes,
Sharp as pain in the light.
And when I walk the whole damn house is mine.

And sometimes at noon in the valley,
In the grass cut over and over in the sunlight,
In the hefted shapes of the stones of the terraces,
Heavy as my own body to lift, I am seen—
In the dirty knuckles and fists of the roots,
Where I lay forgotten till I came back
And grew in the arms of the muscadine,
Twisted and clenched from the neck on down.
Look at these swollen, bloody fists.
This whole damn place here is mine.

Farm Builders

Watkins: Frank, are your poems like children, in that you like all of them the same?

Manley: No. (Laughter.)

Watkins: They're not?

Manley: No, some of them I think are not as good as others.

Watkins: I asked that so that I can give you a choice. If you don't mind, I would like to talk about either "Ghost" or "Going Out." Do you have a preference between the two poems?

Manley: Well, "Ghost" is one that I think doesn't work as well as I would like it to. These are deformed children. (Laughing.)

Watkins: I don't believe it. They're not deformed to me.

Manley: No? Not to you. Well, let's talk about "Ghost" then. That's shorter.

Watkins: What is the setting?

Manley: The setting is Ellijay, Georgia, out in the country. At my place up in north Georgia.

Watkins: Your house?

Manley: Right.

Watkins: Who is Ben Mathis? You say that it's for Ben Mathis.

Manley: Ben Mathis was the man who built that house, who lived on the place. He was my neighbor's cousin. I've met some of his children who have come back to visit, to see the house and examine it—and some of his grandchildren. The only thing I know about him is that somebody said they met him one time scything an orchard up in the cove field, and he had a long white beard.

Watkins: So he was an old-timer.

Manley: Right. He was the one who actually built the house, using some of the materials from an old log house that stood right behind it.

Watkins: Well, is he the ghost?

Manley: Yes.

Watkins: I disagree. (Laughter.)

Manley: (Laughter.) Well, he's the *main* ghost.

Watkins: You ought to have made the title plural.

Manley: "Ghosts"? Well, I guess I should have.

Watkins: Don't joke with me. You really admit that?

Manley: Well, no, I like "Ghost," period. One ghost. I think what I'm talking about is singular. I'm talking about being made into a ghost.

Watkins: I was taking the ghost as the poet or the persona.

Manley: Right.

Watkins: The persona is not Ben Mathis.

Manley: Yes.

Watkins: What's happening in the first three lines?

Manley: All right, it's a conflation of the two. . . . (Laughter.) It's me and Ben Mathis. As I do work there I come in contact with Ben Mathis, and he rises up, his ghostly presence comes there to me.

Watkins: But that's still on the abstract level, and we come back to my question. What's happening in the first three lines?

Manley: The first three lines are talking primarily about Ben Mathis having built that house and being still in it. His labor is still present in it.

Watkins: This is where I know you personally and read the poem personally. I took it to be your rebuilding the porch.

Manley: It is that, too.

Watkins: Conflation.

Manley: Yes, right.

Watkins: In the first place you had your own distinct identity in those three lines, but you associated yourself with the first builder.

Manley: Yes.

Watkins: And you were the second builder.

Manley: I don't know in the first three lines who is the person speaking.

Watkins: Is it both?

Manley: Maybe that's the thing to say; it is *both*.

Watkins: Is the persona you? Who is the persona? The builder, or you at the time of rebuilding, or you at the time of writing?

Manley: (Laughing.) I can't say, really, you know.

Watkins: Could you have said *then* better than now—when you wrote it?

Manley: I don't think so, because I don't . . . I wasn't thinking in those discrete terms. What I was thinking of was this. Let me run on a little bit, and maybe I can put it better in my own words. I was taking the same steps Ben Mathis took to build the house. I took the same steps to rebuild it, you see. So that what I was experiencing was what he experienced.

Watkins: Right. Now what is the time element of the word in the third line, "still"?

Manley: That his muscles were the thing that put it there, and his muscles are still there, holding it up.

Watkins: What about you?

Manley: Me, too.

Watkins: At what time, you? At the time of the holding it up, or at the time of the composition of the poem?

Manley: At the time of the holding up, I think. What happened was that a lot of this fell down, so I had to re-do the thing he did.

Watkins: You're saying, "The muscles of my back still hold it up," and so it has a continuation. It goes right down to the moment of the poem.

Manley: That's right. That's interesting.

Watkins: What is the elemental importance of what you're doing in the first three lines and what Ben Mathis did?

Manley: It's like a poem of Galway Kinnell's. I didn't think of his poem when I wrote this, but it's a poem that explains it.

Watkins: Who's Galway Kinnell?

Manley: He has a poem about porcupines, that they come in and they eat things that people have sweated on. Whatever tastes of human sweat they eat up. So they're destructive forces. I mean this as the opposite of that. In this, the work you do, the things you put yourself into, in some way live after you, and you can come in contact with another person who has done that work by doing the same work.

Watkins: However, it seems to me there is also an element in this poem of building a house, and it can apply to a house and poetry. I think you were getting back to the elemental. You were thinking of craftsman and builder rather than artist. But artist may be included.

Manley: It may be.

Watkins: That would be accident.

Manley: That's right. It would be accident. I was just concerned with the way I was redoing what somebody else in the past had done. And in doing that I came into contact with his ghost.

Watkins: When did you first learn that connection? While you were repairing the porch or afterward? In other words, is this "emotion recollected in tranquility"?

Manley: Yes.

Watkins: You didn't think it at the time. You were sweating too hard. You didn't have *any* of it in your mind at the time. You enjoyed a sort of unconscious physical pleasure in building at the moment.

Manley: No. I think it was a number of doings and redoings. I thought that somebody had been here before me, like on the front sill of the house there are little figures drawn by children. And way back under the house, by the chimney, in the dirt, I found a little toy ladder.

Watkins: Made out of wood?

Manley: Made out of wood. And I found doll heads way up under other places where things had fallen.

Watkins: Now, culturally, country children did play under the house a lot in the time when this was built. We have three different times here. The repairing, the thinking about it, and the writing about it. You said that there was not much of your emotion during the time of repairing. Was there more emotion in the thinking or the writing, or can you compare those?

Manley: The emotion and the thinking and the writing about it were a kind of putting together of all the discrete experiences where I had run into the presence of someone else there before me.

Watkins: What is the moment of greatest emotional intensity in the whole process?

Manley: I can't remember, Floyd.

Watkins: Do you remember how long it took this poem to develop before you picked up a pen?

Manley: It didn't take any time. It just was there, and I started writing it out.

Watkins: I see.

Manley: One thing. This is a poem about history in some ways. You think of north Georgia as a place having no history—I do—it's just woods.

Watkins: You do, or did?

Manley: That's the way I generally thought of it. And there's some of it that's so wooded that you think that people never put a foot there, but what I kept bumping into on this place was the presence of people.

Watkins: How do your hands still shape the water of the spring?

Manley: Of course they don't do it literally. My hands shaped the boards that shape the water.

Watkins: You made the boards?

Manley: I put the boards together that made the trough. It makes the water do what the trough makes the water do. And in that sense I'm still there.

Watkins: Then how is the pine molded? It looks to me as if would be nailed rather than molded. Did you mold and shape by nailing the boards together?

Manley: That's what I intended.

Watkins: Is this word ambiguous? I took it to be an old-time trough made by somebody, say, like Ben Mathis that had been there for a long time. There was mold on it.

Manley: Well, now, that's true. The mold is on it.

Watkins: Are you saying that now, or did you think of it then?

Manley: I can't remember what I thought of then, but I thought of molded as something molded by hand.

Watkins: But the sense of being molded *now* is very much in the poem whether you knew it at the time or not.

Manley: It is. Because that thing is just covered with mold.

Watkins: Was it covered with mold when you wrote the poem?

Manley: I think it must have been, but I don't think I was consciously aware of it.

Watkins: You aren't punning?

Manley: No.

Watkins: Consciously.

Manley: Not consciously.

Watkins: This is an accidental pun?

Manley: It must be.

Watkins: But very meaningful.

Manley: Very meaningful, and I think that it may be that it was an unconscious meaning, you know. Consciously, I moved from "shaped" to "molded," and I was trying to get, I think, the idea that this trough was made out of boards. But maybe Ben Mathis really carved his with some kind of primitive tool.

Watkins: We've already stated that there is a connection between building a house, repairing the porch, and shaping the waters of the spring.

Manley: Right.

Watkins: What happens in the lines about the wires and the windowpanes?

Manley: That moves more directly toward me than Ben Mathis. There were windowpanes in the house, and there was wiring or some sort in there, but there was no electricity in there when I got it.

Watkins: But there were *not* windowpanes in some places.

Manley: There were no windows or panes in a lot of places. No windows in some places, and no panes in others. What happens here is that the double person that you have at the beginning becomes more single in these lines. That happens in the poem; sometimes I come to the fore and sometimes Ben Mathis comes to the fore.

Watkins: Somehow I think that the images are very clear, the meaning is very clear, but the whole thing is a little bit hard to see for a reader. I wonder if that was deliberate.

Manley: Yes.

Watkins: Why would you want that to be deliberate?

Manley: Because I wanted the idea of ghosts to be ghostly. "Ghostly" isn't exactly the word I'd really want to use. I did want the image of a ghost to be the dominant image of the poem, and I did want something hard to see—felt and yet seen to be there, too. So I wanted it to come and go. And I also wanted an ambiguity between me and Ben Mathis. Sometimes I'm talking about him, and sometimes I'm talking about me.

Watkins: What are you trying to define in the ownership of the house in the last line of the first stanza, "And when I walk the whole damn house is mine"?

Manley: I was thinking of the walking as the ghost walking.

Watkins: That's Ben Mathis.

Manley: Well, it's him and me, and so when we walk, that is the both of us. You know you say "The ghost walks tonight" in the horror movies. That's what I meant by "walk" in part, but I also meant me walking. It's the sense of the pride of accomplishment. And also the sense that the things you do live after you.

Watkins: So this is still Ben Mathis's house as well as yours.

Manley: Right. Teilhard de Chardin says he believes that the things that we do don't die completely.

Watkins: Oh; that's Addie Bundren, too, in William Faulkner's *As I Lay Dying.*

Manley: He says even the things that we do with our hands—

Watkins: But that's what you built. How then are you shaped in the grass, or seen in the grass and the shapes of the stones?

Manley: Well, you know on that place there's that cove field where it's really like a European field. It's hand made. There was a stream valley. And what they did, they levelled off that valley with mule scrapes, and they built those terraces. The first one was about six or seven feet high. They rock-faced it to step it down, and it's like five great giant steps, to cut the erosion. That was all row-cropped at that time. So I was thinking about Ben Mathis making the field and making those terraces. I was thinking, too, in the grass cut over and over in the sunlight, again of me cutting that grass because I've done that an awful lot, and of him up in that field with a scythe—and a white beard. There are a lot of those rock walls.

Watkins: So you are in it. "Heavy as my own body." That's you and Ben Mathis, but you're in it because you cut the grass as well as pondered over it and wrote poetry about it.

Manley: Right. But he's in it. I'm in it mostly in the first two lines in the cutting of the grass over and over and over because I've done that so often. He's in it mostly in the building of the terraces, though I have rebuilt some of those where some of your brother's cattle knocked them off. I've put the rocks back up.

Watkins: I see—with a great deal of resentment toward my brother. (Laughter.)

Manley: No. No. (Laughing.) But you know how a cow'll do that; it'll just go down there and knock them down.

Watkins: Explain the lines about the dirty knuckles and being forgotten.

Manley: I guess I'm moving now into the idea of the body that had been working and doing all this stuff, being buried in the earth. I was thinking too of the way roots look. I've planted some fruit trees and some grapevines and things like that up there, and the roots look like fingers and knuckles and fists, like the hands that were making the house and the terraces. I wanted to get an image of resurrection, you know, here at the end. And this is where the poem doesn't work for me as well as it might—because I don't think the image of resurrection quite comes through.

Watkins: What's the problem with it? That it is too natural and not sufficiently supernatural?

Manley: I've never talked to anybody about this; so I don't know. I feel that I don't have any control over the last four lines. One is that I wanted an image of a kind of crucifixion.

Watkins: So you did want a Christian image rather than a natural rebirth?

Manley: I wanted both. I wanted the idea of—you know how grapevines when they're stretched out on the trellises look like arms on a cross? I wanted the idea of being, doing, accomplishing something through pain. Hard work is painful. I wanted that. But I also wanted the swollen and bloody fists to be the grapes themselves, and I'm not certain that comes through. I wanted the arms to burst out into the swollen and bloody fists. The fists are used to do all the stuff he did on the place. All the hard labor involved. I also wanted the image of a grape cluster to be there. I don't know that works in the poem.

Watkins: I didn't see it.

Manley: That's what I'm afraid of.

Watkins: But now I'm not sure but what that is an instance of confinement within space, and I'm not sure that you could build an image so complex as to do all those things at once within that much confinement.

Manley: That may be. And it may be too contrived, too intellectualized, and not what you would call intuitive enough. I think I may have been trying to push the poem a little hard at that point. I think it was a good idea, but for some reason I wasn't able to find a natural, graceful way for it to be done.

Watkins: I think you're hard on yourself.

Manley: Well, maybe. I worked awful hard on that ending, trying to get it to come out the way I wanted it to.

Watkins: Has anything happened in the poem between the last line of the first stanza ("And when I walk the whole damn house is mine") and the last line of the second stanza ("This whole damn place here is mine")? What has happened to change those lines though they resemble each other, or have you already told what did happen?

Manley: I think I probably have already told: what happened in the house itself and with the house itself happens to the landscape around the house. It's made, too.

Watkins: So really the last line is much more comprehensive than the first.

Manley: Yes. It's like he has a kingdom, you know.

Watkins: Oh, that's good. Is it a selfishness in you to claim so much rather arrogantly—"This whole damn place is mine"—or does the conversation we've had suggest that the ego has disappeared into many larger things?

Manley: I would hope it has. I hope that I'm not speaking of myself, but I'm largely speaking of Ben Mathis. I'm also speaking of the way in which anyone puts himself into anything.

Watkins: History, process, religion—everything.

Manley: Right. And the way in which if you put yourself into something it becomes yours. But it's only because you've put yourself into it. It's not because you took some money out of your pocket and put it down and got a deed to a place that makes it yours.

Watkins: What's the difference now between the poem and what it was when you first wrote it? How many drafts did you write?

Manley: It went quickly. I didn't write many drafts. It went quickly until the ending, and when I hit the ending it was like hitting a stone wall. I wrote and messed around with the ending a lot, and I'm not pleased with it. I finally abandoned it.

Watkins: Do you have the manuscript versions of what you threw away?

Manley: I don't think so.

Watkins: That's a great loss, I think.

Manley: Yes. Maybe.

Watkins: I would like to see you groping for it, in those manuscripts.

Manley: I did a lot of groping.

Watkins: In your future writing, save the manuscripts, will you?

Manley: (Laughter). All right.

Watkins: When you become a Nobel Prize winner, I . . .

Manley: Yes. (Laughter). They'll be useful then.

Watkins: Do you see anything you would like to change now?

Manley: I wouldn't know how to change it.

Watkins: I wouldn't even want it changed.

Manley: What bothers me, I think, is that I'm afraid that when you see these swollen and bloody fists you think of only swollen and bloody fists and not of grapes. I don't have a way to force the reader into the grapes.

Watkins: Did you hope that the grapes might be related in any way to communion wine?

Manley: I hadn't thought of that. I knew I was dealing with some resurrection image related to the crucifixion, related to death and rebirth, but I didn't think of communion wine.

Watkins: Consciously.

Manley: Not consciously; that's right. Not consciously.

Watkins: I planned to ask you whether you have shown the poem to Ben Mathis, but obviously dear Ben has departed. You know the character of the builder of that place and the character of those Gilmer County people. They would not admit to a liking for poetry because they don't know that it is called poetry when they read it in the Bible. But if you could jump the barrier of their not knowing poetry and the barrier perhaps of Ben's not being able to read your book—if you could tell this poem as old tale-tellers did—to Ben Mathis and to Ben Mathis as he represents the people you know up there, what do you think his reaction would be.

Manley: I think his reaction would be the same as anyone's.

Watkins: Do you think that Ben Mathis, perhaps illiterate, certainly unaware of poetry, might have a spirit deep enough to comprehend what you also felt?

Manley: Oh, yes.

Watkins: These feelings don't belong only to intellectuals like you?

Manley: I think everybody feels things like that. Poetry is an intellectual pursuit in that you have to know that kind of expression of those feelings.

Watkins: From what you saw in the ladders and the dolls and the faces and the stone walls and the terraces, and all the things that had been done, do you think the man building that place was in a way sharing the craftsmanship of you as builder of the porch and of you as poet?

Manley: Of course, he wasn't consciously sharing it.

Watkins: Well, he was consciously feeling it. He was saying, "I feel damn good about this wall that I built." He was feeling, "This whole damn place is mine."

Manley: Yes, yes.

Watkins: I've made and remolded what God made.

Manley: Right. I see what you mean.

Watkins: I doubt that he ever said it.

Manley: Right.

Watkins: You were feeling it for him when you did it.

Manley: Yes, that's right. Everyone has the feelings and emotions that are present in poetry.

Watkins: All but the demonic and evil.

Manley: Well, maybe that, too. (Laughter.)

Watkins: Oh, really?

Manley: (Laughs.) Yes. But I think that most people are bottled up and don't have the means to express it.

Watkins: The great means of expressing it for the people of that time was the Bible, which often expressed it for them. Especially the King James Bible.

Manley: And hymns and religious experiences.

Watkins: We have left out one thing. Once we have reached this articulation of the ways you work, then we have to drop it and go back and read the poem and forget the conscious statement of the things we have said and feel again the poem as it is. If you don't do that then you are subject to the constant charge of tearing the poem apart, which is unjust to it. But once you have done this and go back to the poem, then it can exist in a greater fullness than it ever has had before.

Manley: Yes, but I think the poem is different for me from what it is for someone else.

Watkins: You think it's different for you from what it is for me?

Manley: When I say in some lines it's more Ben Mathis and in others it's more me than Ben Mathis—the way in which one comes to the fore and one recedes, now, I think that happens for me, but it doesn't happen for you.

Watkins: I think it happens for me after you told me. Now maybe the only full experience of this poem—the only full understanding of this poem can come perhaps to a person who has known you, that house, your history in that place.

Manley: Probably so.

Watkins: A reader who does not know Ellijay and does not know Frank Manley may never know the fullness of it.

Going Out

Outside the house
year after year
the rot inside each drop of rain
inside the friction of the wind
the smell of a cellar
the color of lichens on stone
the light coming through
from inside the boards
like light in a wasp nest
and the house going back
inside the storm
inside the tearing
the grinding of tin

Inside the house
something had happened
something got loose and stayed inside
in the hole of the chimney
something was there
the walls ripped and hanging in sheets
the pile of dirty clothes in the corner
something had torn it with knives
and was there
in the shattered glass on the floor
sharp as hate

And on the wall
a sign
like a suicide note
saying

WE GOING OUT
AND ETERNATY
TO MEET GOD

RU READY
GODS CLOCK IS TICKING
AWAY ITS TIME

saying o yes
we all going out
after the murder
after the last knife of the looting
the rape of the old clothes of our body
we going out
for god's clock is ticking
inside the rain
scratching the wasp nest wall of our skull
god's clock is ticking
inside the wind of our lives
inside the wind of our breath
god's clock is ticking
inside the storms
that sweep around us at night
with the screeching of tin
that rips at the top of our skull
god's clock is ticking
inside the shine of our bones
burning inside us
and we going out
o yes we going out
we all going out of that house

We All Going Out

Watkins: Obviously the center of the poem is the sign. Did you invent it, or did you see such a sign somewhere?

Manley: In a tenant house, an abandoned tenant house somewhere between Atlanta and Columbia, South Carolina.

Watkins: What kind of country?

Manley: Well, it's all like around Atlanta here, kind of Piedmont, you know. Columbia is right on the fall line.

Watkins: Where was the sign in the house?

Manley: Tacked on the wall. My wife likes to go look at old houses when nobody's living in them; so we stopped and went into that one, and there was the sign. It's written in some kind of red—not crayon because it runs a little bit. Rain has made it run a little. It's on the back of a Post Toasties box.

Watkins: Really?

Manley: Yes. It was hanging on the wall. The house was full of debris, mattresses and stuff that you find in those houses sometimes.

Watkins: And you stole it.

Manley: I took it off the wall. (Laughter.)

Watkins: Did you follow the writer's lines or did you change them?

Manley: I thought I followed them, but I can't remember. I know I didn't put periods after *R U*. The sign says capital *R*, capital *U*.

Watkins: He also has a period after *To*. To. Meet God.

Manley: I wasn't concerned about reproducing it exactly.

Watkins: You didn't follow his lines. [Looks at sign on wall of office.] He's got "we going out *and*" and you've got "we going out." It's curious how he has spacing on that sign that's like stanzas, isn't it? Is that because he hit the end of the box, or do you think he might have had rhythm or stanza in mind?

Manley: I think he may have had line breaks in mind. We keep saying "he." It could have been a woman, you know. (Laughter.)

Watkins: (Silence)

Manley: Could have been a child.

Watkins: I think it'd be a very mature child. In his thinking. He's already been moved religiously in some fashion.

Manley: What impressed me about it was the way they moved out of the house—into eternity. They had abandoned it.

Watkins: And the minute they move out physically it becomes metaphorical.

Manley: Yes.

Watkins: He ran out of space at the bottom too.

Manley: Yes, right.

Watkins: You did not follow his stanzas at all.

Manley: No, I didn't. I can see that now. I don't know why I didn't.

Watkins: Did you have stanzas of your own in mind?

Manley: I probably did. I probably broke it the way I wanted to. I can't see stanzas in the sign.

Watkins: I don't care whether you call them stanzas, paragraphs, or breaks, but I take it that there's a break after "eternaty" and after "ready." Look at the interesting "REAdy" there—capital R-E-A and small *dy*. Is that ignorance or childhood?

Manley: I would guess it is ignorance.

Watkins: We're talking about ignorance of writing, not necessarily ignorance of spiritual conditions.

Manley: That's right.

Watkins: What does "AND ETERNATY" mean?

Manley: I don't know what "and" means. I took it to mean "to eternity." "We're going out to eternity," literally.

Watkins: I see.

Manley: What it literally says, I guess, is that we're going out and, having gone out, we'll be in eternity.

Watkins: He could have meant we're going out *and* as we go out eternity is moving in on us.

Manley: That could be. I don't know what it means.

Watkins: What does a ticking clock mean to the persona, or you, in the poem?

Manley: Well, it seems to me that you have a certain amount of time. That time is always passing, and for the individual time will end. You will die, and then you will meet God.

Watkins: Do you think this person had lain, maybe, half-awake, or awake, hearing a psychologically awful affecting ticking of a clock?

Manley: No. I just think they thought of death as like a time bomb, or the end of your life as a time bomb. Something that's ticking away.

Watkins: Have you ever been psychologically affected by one of those old loud mechanical ticking clocks?

Manley: Not psychologically affected. But I've been kept awake by them. Is that what you mean?

Watkins: Oh, I've gotten frightened by them.

Manley: Really? Have you? I never have.

Watkins: I've counted my life passing away by a clock ticking.

Manley: Well, it may be something like that was standing behind this. I don't know.

Watkins: In him, not in you?

Manley: No, not in me. I thought it was more like a time bomb. That it was ticking away and that there was going to come this big explosion.

Watkins: I would have thought of a quiet ending, when the clock quit.

Manley: Is that right? No, I thought of a time bomb, tick, tick, ticking . . . and BOOM; it was going to really blow up into a big thing when you moved out into eternity and met God face to face.

Watkins: Well, let's grant that's in the poem. The clock could mean three different things to the three of us—me, you, and that person—is that right?

Manley: I can't stand behind that sign. I don't know what in the world it is. It was affecting to me to see it in the place I saw it.

Watkins: Why was it affecting, Frank?

Manley: Because it was as though those people had left their earthly home, you know, and it was wrecked and abandoned. They had gone into eternity, and this was the sign that said that's where they were going.

Watkins: I take it to be the moving experience of a religious fundamentalist who is not well educated but powerfully moved by religion in a way nobody understands.

Manley: But I don't think it's just restricted to the fundamentalist.

Watkins: Oh, I don't, either.

Manley: What this sign reminds me of—the reason I keep it in my office—is to remember that there is a different kind of time that I need to be aware of. I get tied up in my daily activities, and I forget time and the consequences of time. I forget the really important things easily.

Watkins: Does God have a different clock from man?

Manley: Yes, I think so.

Watkins: When you are running by your clock, it's very likely you're ignoring God's clock.

Manley: Yes. It's not my clock. I don't like to think of it as my clock. I'd rather go with the other clock.

Watkins: It is your clock and you're running by it even though you don't like to think about it.

Manley: I think of it more as society's clock.

Watkins: That's the one that compels you to come to school in the morning.

Manley: Right.

Watkins: But it is still society's clock. It determines your clock.

Manley: Well, yes. If you choose to let it. I feel like I have a kind of choice. More than that. I don't think that my clock is this and God's clock is that.

Watkins: What do you—what can the reader—make of the difference between the illiteracy, the condition of the home, the whole basic, poverty-stricken life and the profundity of religion in that setting?

Manley: I can't speak sociologically. I can only speak as an outsider looking in, and I've been impressed with this over and over—with southern fundamental religion—that it recalls me to a real sense of fervor and significance.

Watkins: No matter education.

Manley: Right. No matter education.

Watkins: That person's sociological, economic condition does not determine his religion. He can feel as deeply as you with a Ph. D.

Manley: Yes. That's right. That's right. I think what I see in the fundamentalist is a kind of commitment to religion that is lacking in a lot of other places. Religion is really a central experience—not a peripheral one—not on the edges, on Sunday. A religious experience is not being a member of a social club.

Watkins: Do you feel any displeasure when you see a highway sign "Prepare to Meet Jesus"?

Manley: No, no. No, no.

Watkins: I do.

Manley: Do you? I don't. I'm moved by it.

Watkins: What do you feel about it when you see it on a car?

Manley: A little less on a car, but when I see it painted on a rock, or something like that, I think somebody like a prophet has been there.

Watkins: This may be a condemnation of me, but I'm afraid it's a cheap prophet.

Manley: No, I don't think so. I think it's a man who is outside the kind of social clock that we were talking about, outside society's clock.

Watkins: He's painting by God's clock when he paints on that rock.

Manley: That's right. He's moving by God's clock. That's right. He's moving according to his deepest beliefs and deepest commitment. And I admire it.

Watkins: And you attribute the same feeling to this sign.

Manley: Yes.

Watkins: Your first two stanzas are structured by "outside the house" and "inside the house."

Manley: Right.

Watkins: Why do you begin with outside the house and inside the house, and what's the difference?

Manley: I think outside the house what's happening is the slow process of decay. And inside the house something violent has occurred.

Watkins: What's rotting outside the house?

Manley: Just the body of the house.

Watkins: You say the rot's inside the drop of rain.

Manley: That's because the rain brings the rot to the house.

Watkins: The rot is in the house caused by the drop of rain.

Manley: Caused by the drop of rain, right. Caused by its existence in time. It's just going to rot.

Watkins: How does that proceed to the smell of a cellar?

Manley: I always thought of rot as smelling like cellars. Mildewy, damp. What I also wanted, Floyd, was the idea of moving toward the house. You see the outside first; and then you move inside and see the violence that occurred; then you see the sign, like a process or a movement inward.

Watkins: Which is much more than merely entering a strange house; it is also entering into the inner sensation of a soul.

Manley: Right, right. What I'm thinking, too, is metaphorical. This house represents a kind of individual.

Watkins: You looked at the house as something like the human body. That's a common figure in poetry.

Manley: Very common. And the violence. I don't know exactly what I mean by the violence, but I guess I mean something like Thomas More says: He says that when you feel pain, like a heart attack or something like that, it's no different from knives being put through you or no different from any kind of torture that can be inflicted on you.

Watkins: You mean from an acid stomach or something like that?

Manley: No. A heart attack. The pain from a heart attack is no different, he said, from torture or taking knives and putting them through you, or breaking your knuckles. He said arthritis is no different from that. There are natural pains in the body as intense as any kind of torture. I was thinking of that kind of violence. That's part of it. I don't know what else I was thinking. I guess I was thinking of death as a kind of intense violence.

Watkins: How is the house in the first stanza going back inside the storm?

Manley: It came out of things in Nature—like boards, trees, and so on, and now it's reverting to nature again.

Watkins: That's a powerful image of the tearing. "Inside the tearing/ the grinding of tin." That's the violence of going back into the original condition. God's time is working through the storm and the tearing and the grinding of the tin. Ultimately.

Manley: Right. It's the process.

Watkins: Now tell me about inside the house.

Manley: Well, that's what I was just saying. That inside the house some violence has occurred.

Watkins: What's in the hole in the chimney?

Manley: I don't know.

Watkins: Now is that a hole in the chimney, or is that the chimney itself being a hole?

Manley: Well, what I meant was that there is a sense of violence loose in the house that's still there. You can see it in the hole that's been knocked in the chimney.

Watkins: Oh, so there has been a hole knocked in the chimney, rather than the chimney just being a hole.

Manley: Yes. A hole knocked in the chimney. Like, you know, in old houses a lot of times you go into them and somebody has dug up the hearth looking for money. That kind of violence has occurred.

Watkins: What was the purpose of ripping and hanging—the walls ripping and hanging in sheets. And the knives cutting the clothes and the shattered glass. They all show destruction, but do they have a meaning like searching for money?

Manley: Well, literally, you go into a lot of old houses and they've glued paper on the walls, and it's fallen off.

Watkins: Even newspapers. Have you ever seen that?

Manley: Right. Newspapers and that sort of thing. It's just a literal description, but it also suggests ripping and tearing and violence.

Watkins: In the first stanza what is the "light in a wasps' nest"?

Manley: If you were to take a light and put it inside a wasps' nest, it would be kind of translucent. I suppose really I should have said hornets' nest. That's what I was thinking of. The kind of thing made of bits of wood that the insect has masticated. What I meant was the idea of wood drawn so thin that you could see through it, but still wood.

Watkins: Do the images of the final stanza connect with the images of the first two?

Manley: Oh, yes. Yes. Sure. The violence, the rape, the looting, the knife, the rain, the wasp nest wall of our skull—it all runs back.

Watkins: You're thinking of a sort of honeycombed bone skull with the flesh gone?

Manley: Well, I'm thinking of something like a light inside it, too.

Watkins: What's the light inside?

Manley: The head or brain.

Watkins: I know, but what is the light metaphorically?

Manley: Intelligence, consciousness.

Watkins: Existence, even soul?

Manley: Maybe. I don't know. I don't know that I specified in my own mind what it would be. I wanted the third stanza to come out of seeing the sign and getting a realization. The realization is implicit in the first two stanzas, that the house equals the human body. Then the sign is seen, and *then* the speaker fully realizes that the house is like the human body and that we are going out, and we are going to have happen to us what the sign says. And so the poem then ties itself together in that realization. I also wanted that last stanza to read like a preacher.

Watkins: As a Catholic, does your high church Catholicism have anything to do with the low church fundamentalism of the writer of the note? You don't have any kind of patronizing high church attitude toward the religious—

Manley: Oh, no, no, no. Just the opposite. I have great admiration. I think that what happens a lot of times in high church Anglicanism, high church anything, high church Presbyterianism, is that people lose sight of religion and the real religious experience for other things—for the ritual, for singing in the choir, for meeting all the people who belong to the church, and so on, and therefore they miss the point. They're not really outside society, and I see this sign and all the rest of it as outside society. I tend to think of this poem as dealing with fundamentalism in a different way but related to Flannery O'Connor. It's the same kind of subject, you know. I think that she both admires and feels a little alien to this kind of religious experience. I tend to admire it and not feel that alien to it.

Watkins: I agree. Have you thought of the genre or form of this poem? That is to say, have you thought whether it's lyric, dramatic, or narrative?

Manley: No, I haven't. I think of it, I guess, as a kind of Victorian poem. I went there and I thought this. I went there and I saw that and I thought this. A lot of poems are like that. If I were to think of a form for it, it'd be like that.

Watkins: I thought of it as having elements of the lyrical, the dramatic, and the narrative—all were in it.

Manley: That's probably true. There is a narrative structure, and there is a lyrical sense that comes out of the narrative structure.

Watkins: In your confrontation of the mind in print, there's a kind of relationship between you and the person who wrote the sign.

Manley: That's right.

Watkins: Do you think an awareness of type of poetry is helpful to a reader?

Manley: I don't know.

Watkins: I believe it helps him: by classifying, he sees things that you felt. Let's go back. You did try to write the last stanza as a preacher preaches.

Manley: The funny thing about it is, no, I didn't.

Watkins: Oh!

Manley: I didn't. No. This gets into how I wrote a lot of these poems. What I tend to do is write very quickly in first draft. The first version tends to be very long, and some parts of it are very hot and some parts of it are cold. Well, I wrote a long first draft of this poem. Blocked out maybe two single-spaced pages. And parts of it were good, and parts of it weren't good, but there was a block at the end that was almost just that last stanza as it stands. And it sounded like a preacher.

Watkins: You discovered it sounded like a preacher after you'd already written it?

Manley: Yes, right.

Watkins: And was the whole poem fast, or just the last part?

Manley: You mean, in the writing?

Watkins: Yes.

Manley: The last part I didn't touch.

Watkins: Oh, you never revised a word?

Manley: I never revised a word of that. The last stanza just . . .

Watkins: How much did you revise the first part?

Manley: A good bit. I did the outside-inside division after I had it down.

Watkins: That was before you'd gotten into the spirit of the religion of it, the salvation of it, wasn't it?

Manley: No, I wrote it all drafted out at the same time. And in the first draft that last stanza was there fully developed. And it was the first part that I had to form and get right.

Watkins: How long did you spend revising the first part? A few sittings or would you revise a line and come back in a day or two and revise another line?

Manley: There'd be a few sittings. I just piddled with it. There was a rape in there at one time, and I had a mattress as the body and things like that. You know, just details. The overall conception was there. Rot and then violence. But then it was just working out the details. Deciding which details I wanted, and getting rid of the ones I didn't want. I dickered with the first part a lot. I didn't have to do much with the last part. Maybe because of the subject, I just fell into the personality of a preacher, and that's why it sounds like it. Or maybe I was just modeling myself on one while I was writing it.

Watkins: But you weren't saying, I will model myself; you weren't even aware of it; you got through with it, and then you said, By God (laughter). . . .

Manley: By God . . . (Laughter.)

Watkins: By God, preacher, this is very much like you.

Manley: That's right, yes.

Watkins: When you approached this interview, did you think that I would have found the preacher in the last stanza?

Manley: I figured you would, yes.

Watkins: I had to read it two or three times before I saw the preacher. Do you think our colleagues who are from the North would find the country preacher in there?

Manley: I don't know. It depends on whether they've had any exposure to that kind of preaching. Some churches in the North do have transplanted southerners doing that kind of preaching.

Watkins: You think a man without exposure might well not catch it?

Manley: Right.

Watkins: Well, what did you put it there for then? Did you put it there for the man who had been exposed? What did you hope that the man who had not been exposed would get?

Manley: Well, like I say, I wasn't thinking of a preacher, at first. I was just trying to get down the feeling that this thing created in me, and I fell into the rhythm and into the language of a preacher to express that.

Watkins: You did it for yourself then?

Manley: I did it to get it out.

Watkins: When you published the poem, were you hoping

that the editor and the readers might catch this fundamentalist rhythm?

Manley: No, it wasn't significant that they did. It was what was said that was most important to me. And the fact that it was rhythmic was important. The pattern of rhythm was right, and I was imitating, I'm sure, probably unconsciously, the patterns I'd heard preachers like this fall into. But the pattern was right.

Watkins: I think the two rhythms might merge, don't you? God's clock and the preacher's?

Manley: Might very well.

Watkins: Tell me about the Gasper.

Manley: There's a church near us—New Liberty Baptist Church—about two miles from us in Ellijay, and lots of our neighbors go to it. We went with our children one time, the first experience I ever had with this, and the preacher was known as a Gasper. He would say two or three lines—he was inspired by the Holy Spirit—say two or three lines and gasp.

Watkins: Do you mean lines?

Manley: Well, I mean he would say two or three phrases or words and gasp. It was a peculiar experience. I'd never heard anything like that, and I'm not thinking of that kind of preacher here, a Gasper—not quite that extreme—but a man who is inspired by the Spirit.

Watkins: Why do you think, in that man's heart, he gasps? Was it emotional and spiritual, or rhetorical, or unconscious?

Manley: Oh, I think it was rhetorical, an attempt to get into the spirit. And you know, that's an—

Watkins: To work himself up?

Manley: To work himself—to keep himself worked up, right.

Watkins: To shout? Like they shout?

Manley: Right.

Watkins: Almost verging over into something like what might be for some people the unknown tongues.

Manley: Yes, right. Now, that's in a sense what I was trying to do, Floyd. That's another reason this falls into the preacher. Because what I was trying to do was be inspired when I was writing. I wanted to write this without thinking that I was writing, just let it come out without my consciously shaping it.

Watkins: Is that the reason for no punctuation?

Manley: There's no punctuation in any of it. The whole poem.

Watkins: You know, I had noticed the lack of punctuation only in the last part.

Manley: Is that right? I wanted to let it run over. Now, I can't read this poem. I've tried to read this poem before, and I can't do it because I can't read it the way I hear that last stanza. It should be read like a Gasper, but I'm too inhibited, personally, to really fling it out, the last stanza, the way it ought to be flung.

Watkins: Before either one of us attempts to read it, tell me the devices, as you look on it consciously now, that contribute to the preaching besides lack of punctuation.

Manley: Well, again, I don't know.

Watkins: Weren't you aware of the parallelism of *after the murder* and *after the last?*

Manley: I'm sure I must have been. I think what it is, though, Floyd, is that I wrote this in about a minute and a half or two minutes. So the devices are just there. I think you're right, though, when I go back and look at it. I can see rhythm. I can see parallelism. I can see repetition.

Watkins: Look at the repetition of *we all going out, we going out . . .*

Manley: And *God's clock is ticking.* It's all full of that.

Watkins: *Inside the wind, inside the wind.* What else? I don't guess it's rhetorical that the wasps' nest here is connected to the first part.

Manley: Well, all of it's connected with the screeching.

Watkins: Is the style of the last stanza like the style of the first?

Manley: Oh, no.

Watkins: I see. Do you see anything else that makes it sound like a preacher? The length of phrases does.

Manley: Maybe it does.

Watkins: Does the length of phrases in this stanza correspond with the length of the phrases of the Gasper?

Manley: I don't know. I can't remember the Gasper that well. I've heard radio preachers and I've heard some country preachers—

Watkins: Do a lot of preachers gasp?

Manley: A lot of them up our way do.

Watkins: They gasp, and they phrase, and they—how do they mark a phrase besides gasping? Is there another way?

Manley: Well, they'll bend over, and fling their arms, and you know, squat and pound on things, and that business.

Watkins: That's really a little more primitive than I remember in a long time.

Manley: Yes. Well, I've seen them do that.

Watkins: They even almost expectorate as they reach the end of a phrase. The gasping is really timing their breathing.

Manley: Yes, that's right. That's what it is. Another thing I wanted this poem to do is pick up speed. I wanted there to be a kind of velocity to the poem. I wanted it to be outside and inside, in the sign, and in the emotional experience. The emotions burst out.

Watkins: This poem brought me right back to my childhood when I did hear such preachers, when we visited relatives in the country. And I got so interested I read it to myself. First, I didn't discover it; second, I read it to myself; and third, I have preached it.

Manley: Have you really? (Laughs.)

Watkins: Yes, I have.

Manley: Did you gasp it?

Watkins: No. Do you know that there were a lot of people who had spiritual feelings that made them want to preach? When they weren't preachers? They wished in repentance and regret and temporary religious experience that they were preachers that could preach.

Manley: No, I didn't know that.

Watkins: Now my Great Uncle Bud Wheeler, a drunk and a great, strong, physical man, had a little bitty mule, and his feet when he rode it almost touched the ground. My father heard him on a hilltop one night saying, preaching a sermon when he was drunk, sitting on his mule. And he said, "Here I sit on my mule, preaching the gospel. If I'd had the chance I'd a been a damn good preacher."

Manley: I heard a story kind of like that. There was a preacher, Fowler, lived near us. He became a preacher because one time he went crazy and they found him in the Cartecay River in February, stark naked, up in the mountains, and they carried him off, and he came back as a preacher. He'd never been one before.

Watkins: Have you ever read this poem to a group?

Manley: No, I don't read it. I just can't read it.

Watkins: Would you like to sort of see if I can catch the rhythm?

Manley: Yes. Go ahead.

[Watkins reads last stanza with fervor.]

Manley: (Applauds.) Well, that's really good. That's really good. Now, that's exactly the way I hear it in my own head.

Watkins: You can't do that, though?

Manley: But I can't do it. No, I just can't do it.

Watkins: You haven't heard it as much as I have, have you?

Manley: No, it isn't that. I can hear it, and I know when I hear it. And I've tried to put it down. But I'm just too inhibited. I'd have to have another personality, I think, to really do it out loud.

Watkins: Let me say this, if I can phrase it. We both have the common experience of hearing country preachers. I could read and from your judgment of country preachers you could catch it in the poem and hear it again when I read it. The ultimate tribute we're working for here is not to prove my reading, but to prove the beauty of the catching of the rhythm of the poem.

Manley: Good. For me, personally, it isn't so much the country preacher standing forth at the end of the poem that's important, but rather, what the country preacher says, and the way I could say what the country preacher says best is to say it the way the country preacher said it. I don't want the reader to end the poem thinking, Well, that's a good imitation of a country preacher, but it doesn't mean too much. I want the reader to finish up the poem saying that he has used a country preacher as a vehicle to get at a religious kind of experience that's meaningful.